MODERN U.S.
TANKS & AFVs

MICHAEL GREEN AND GREG STEWART

Dedication

To our good friend Randy Talbot, TACOM staff historian,
for his help and support during the completion of this book.

First published in 2003 by MBI Publishing Company, Galtier Plaza,
Suite 200, 380 Jackson Street, St. Paul, MN 55101-3885 USA

The information in this book is true and complete to the best of
our knowledge. All recommendations are made without any
guarantee on the part of the author or Publisher, who also disclaim
any liability incurred in connection with the use of this data or
specific details.

We recognize that some words, model names and designations,
for example, mentioned herein are the property of the trademark
holder. We use them for identification purposes only. This is not
an official publication.

MBI Publishing Company titles are also available at discounts in bulk
quantity for industrial or sales-promotional use. For details write to
Special Sales Manager at Motorbooks International Wholesalers &
Distributors, Galtier Plaza, Suite 200, 380 Jackson Street, St. Paul,
MN 55101-3885 USA

ISBN 0-7603-1467-5

On the front cover: The crews of two Marine Corps M1A1 Abrams
tanks take a break between training exercises at the Marine Corps
Air Ground Combat Center (MCAGCC) in southern California at
Twentynine Palms. Both tanks have the track-width, mine-clearing
plow fitted. Once attached to the tank, the plows can be raised for
travel or lowered for use within the vehicle. *Greg Stewart*

On the frontispiece: This photo was taken inside the turret of a
Marine Corps M1A1 tank and shows the storage arrangement of
16 of the 34 120mm main gun rounds stored in the vehicle's rear
turret bustle. The main gun rounds are located directly behind the
loader's position and can be removed without the loader leaving
his or her seat. *Greg Stewart*

On the title page: As its designation indicates, the Marine Corps
LAV-25 is armed with the turret-mounted M242 25mm automatic
cannon. It is stabilized in elevation and traverse, which allows it to
be fired accurately while on the move. One of the vehicle's four
scouts stands up in the rear hull of the LAV-25 pictured on a road
at Camp Pendleton, California. *Hans Halberstadt*

On the back cover: This M2A1 Bradley took part in a large-scale
training exercise conducted in West Germany in 1988. The 25mm
automatic cannon in the vehicle's turret can fire single shots or at
selectable rates of fire of 100 or 200 rounds per minute. It fires both
armor-piercing discarding sabot (APDS) rounds or high-explosive
incendiary (HEI) rounds. *Michael Green*

About the authors:
Michael Green and Greg Stewart are freelance writers, researchers,
and photographers. They both specialize in military subjects and
have many books to their credit. This is the fifth book that Green
and Stewart have co-authored. In addition, Green has written
numerous articles for a variety of national and international
military-related magazines, including *Jane's Defense Weekly, Marine
Corps Gazette, Army* magazine, *Armed Forces Journal, Armor*
magazine, *Defense Asia-Pacific, Armada,* and *Wheels and Tracks*
magazine. Green also serves as a board member of the world-
famous Military Vehicle Technology Foundation
(www.milvehtechfound.com) in northern California.

Edited by Amy Glaser
Designed by Kou Lor

Printed in China

CONTENTS

ACKNOWLEDGMENTS

Special thanks are due to the Army and Marine Corps public affairs offices whose support and help made this book possible. Thanks also go to the various program managers and their staffs at the Tank Automotive and Armaments Command (TACOM). Peter Keating, director of communications at General Dynamics Land Systems Division; Herb Muktarian, manager of communications at United Defense Ground Systems Division; and Jim Flynn, director of communications for General Motors Defense, supplied photographs and information for this book.

Other company representatives also helped out with photographs and information, including Craig MacNab, director of communications at AM General. At O'Gara-Hess & Eisenhardt Company, John Mayles, vice-president of military programs; Anthony Crayden, manager of contracts; and Eva Keller, marketing director, were helpful. Our good friend Hans Halberstadt was kind enough to provide photographs and information for this book. Photographs were also acquired from the Defense Visual Information Center (DVIC).

Individuals who made an extra effort to assist the authors in the completion of this work include Colonel Chris Cardine (Ret.), Elizabeth Buscemie, Ron Hare, Huck Hagenbuch, Dick Hunnicutt, and Linda Johnson. Other individuals who took the time to assist the authors include Kathy Vinson, Rob Wurtz, John Boyce, Richard Pierce, Ann and Erik Zetterstrom, and Scott DeCarrillo.

INTRODUCTION

The U.S. Army is currently in the early stages of transforming itself away from heavy ground-weapon systems that have been the centerpiece of its combat power for over a century. The new Army will be a more agile strategic force composed of lighter, readily deployable ground systems that will use new technologies to maintain the lethality and survivability of the current heavy systems.

The Army has adopted a careful three-step approach to the goal of fielding this new class of ground weapon platforms.

The first step is to upgrade some of the existing heavy ground weapon systems the Army refers to as the Legacy Force. This is an ongoing effort within the Army.

The second step is the Interim Force, which is composed of much lighter armored vehicles that can be deployed quickly by air anywhere in the world in a matter of days. The first of these lighter armored vehicles were fielded in 2002.

The third and final step, planned for full implementation by 2020, will be the Objective Force. Most of the weapon systems that will make up the Objective Force presently exist only as computer-rendered drawings or prototypes.

This book presents an overview of the Army's Legacy Force vehicles and the new Interim Force vehicles that will form the core of the Army's ground weapon systems for the next 20 years or more. Some of the armored fighting vehicles currently in use with the U.S. Marine Corps and the U.S. Air Force are also covered.

Many technical details on the armored vehicles covered in this book have been eliminated in order to accommodate size and format restrictions imposed by the publisher. The authors have therefore concentrated on a select group of vehicles and present brief background histories and the paths the vehicles took to their present configurations.

TANKS

M1 Abrams

The cutting edge of U.S. Army armor-protected firepower on today's battlefields is represented by the various versions of the well-known M1 series of Abrams tanks. The vehicle was named in honor of General Creighton W. Abrams. As a lieutenant colonel, Abrams commanded tank units in World War II and later served as chief of staff of the Army.

The Abrams first entered Army service in 1981. The initial version of the Abrams was designated the M1. It was a replacement for the Army's aging M60 series tanks, the last of which retired from Army National Guard service in 1997. The M1 was fitted with the same M68E1 105mm main gun mounted on most of the M60 series.

The original designer and builder of the M1 was the Chrysler Corporation. Due to serious financial problems in the early 1980s, Chrysler was forced to sell its military business in 1982. The government approved the sale to General Dynamics Corporation, which named it the General Dynamics Land System (GDLS) division.

According to recent statements by the Army, various versions of the Abrams will be the main "go to war" platform through 2020. At that point in time, the Army's future Objective Force should be fully fielded. The Army currently refers to the Abrams and other armored fighting vehicles (AFVs) developed during the Cold War era as the Legacy Force. The Legacy Force vehicles helped win the Cold War. It was a heavy force designed to defeat the Soviet-led Warsaw Pact forces with a doctrine that was perfected in peacetime and confirmed in combat during Operation Desert Storm in 1991 and Operation Iraqi Freedom in 2003. The Army is making the transitional move to the Objective Force for many reasons. One is that the Legacy Force is no longer needed, and it wasn't because it was a failure or obsolete in capability. The type of armed conflict envisioned by top American war-fighting planners in the future dictates a lighter, faster, more lethal and technologically advanced force better able to deal with future threat environments than the Legacy Force.

The last production version of the M60 tank series in U.S. Army service was the M60A3. It was first used in 1978. This M60A3 tank belonged to the California Army National Guard (CANG) and took part in a training exercise at Fort Hunter in Liggett, California, in 1992. The CANG has long since replaced its M60A3s with M1A1s. *Michael Green*

Protection

In place of the heavier steel armor that protected the crew of M60-series tanks, M1s are protected on the front and sides by a composite armor array. Since composite armor is not structurally sound, the M1 is encased in steel armor boxes. The armor on the front of the M1 turret is almost two feet thick. The hull skirt side armor is less than three inches thick.

The ingredients that make up the composite armor on the M1 Abrams is a classified military secret. However, by definition, composite armor is a combination of different metals, plastics, and ceramics.

The armor that protects the front and sides of the M1 hull and turret was developed in England and adapted by American engineers for use on the Abrams. The special armor is called Chobham, after the British lab where it was developed.

Chobham armor is very effective against shaped-charge warheads that can easily penetrate the homogeneous steel armors of older vehicles. Shaped-charge warheads are carried by a wide variety of antitank rockets and missiles.

Another important survivability feature of all M1 versions is the compartmentalization of the main gun ammunition in an armored rear turret bustle and armored hull ammunition compartment. Two one-inch-thick steel blast doors separate the turret crew from the rear turret bustle. These blast doors are open only when the Abrams' loader hits a knee switch to remove a main gun round from the ammunition store. Once the loader turns to insert the round into the breech of the main gun and removes his or her knee from the knee switch, the blast doors close automatically. If a projectile were to detonate the ammunition in the bustle box, blow-off panels on the roof of the turret bustle would immediately vent the extremely hot ammunition propellant explosive gases upward and away from the crew.

A U.S. Army M1 tank armed with a 105mm main gun dashes across a West German field in 1984. The suspension system consists of 14 road-wheel stations (seven per side) with steel torsion bars and advanced internal rotary shock absorbers at all positions. *Michael Green*

Taken at the moment of firing, this photograph demonstrates the dramatic fireball created when a round of main-gun ammunition leaves the barrel of the 105mm gun mounted in the M1 tank. The decision to engage a target with the tank's main gun is almost always made by the vehicle commander and not the gunner. *Greg Stewart*

Mobility

A novel departure for the Army was the bold choice to power the M1 with a gas turbine engine. Most postwar American tanks were powered by diesel engines. The Army's decision to use a gas turbine engine in the M1 was heavily influenced by the turbine's light weight and small volume, which allowed more of the vehicle's weight to be allocated to armor protection. Quiet operation and a smokeless exhaust were seen as survivability advantages. The Army also had a maintenance and repair infrastructure to support the gas turbine of the Bell "Huey" helicopter.

Gas turbine engines have a much longer service life between major overhauls than comparable diesel engines. The Army counted on this factor to lower the operation and maintenance cost of its tank fleet.

The biggest disadvantage is that gas turbine engines use more fuel than diesel engines at idle. The Army decided that this disadvantage far outweighed the turbine's many advantages. The fuel mileage between diesel and gas turbine engines is roughly comparable when the vehicles are in motion.

The powerful Honeywell (formerly Textron Lycoming) AGT-1500 (1,500 horsepower) gas turbine engine can propel the roughly 60-ton M1 to speeds of up to 45 miles per hour on paved, level roads. With its advanced torsion bar suspension system, the M1 can achieve speeds of 30 miles per hour over fairly rough

An M1 tank commander has dismounted from his vehicle to confer with a superior officer during a training exercise at Fort Hood, Texas, in 1985. His loader has moved over to the tank commander's cupola to maintain surveillance of the area directly in front of the vehicle. *Michael Green*

terrain. In contrast, the M60 series tanks could make only 30 miles per hour on roads and less than 15 miles per hour over moderately rough terrain.

The AGT-1500 gas turbine engine has served the entire series of Abrams tanks very well over the years, but they are starting to wear out. Since no new AGT-1500 engines have been built since 1992, the Army has depended on overhauled engines from the Anniston Army Depot for its Abrams tank fleet.

In March 2000 the Army officially requested proposals for the development of a new engine for the Abrams series. In 2001, the Army selected the team comprising the turbine engine divisions of Honeywell and General Electric to develop a new gas turbine engine, the LV100-5. The new gas turbine engine is both smaller and lighter than the AGT-1500, yet it has the same 1,500-horsepower rating. The Army authorized $28.6 million in 2002 to fund the Abrams engine replacement program. The LV100-5 is scheduled for production by 2004.

Improving the M1 Abrams: The IPM1 Abrams
Chrysler and General Dynamics built 2,374 M1s between 1980 and 1985. In 1985 and 1986, General

The open breech end of the 105mm main gun and the gunner's position is visible in this photograph of an M1 tank turret. The main gun has a sliding-wedge breech block. The cartridge case ejection is automatic and supplied from recoil energy. *Hans Halberstadt*

A loader on an M1 tank uses his fist to shove a main gun round into the breech of a 105mm main gun. This is done to prevent his fingers from being smashed by the closing of the breech block. *Hans Halberstadt*

Dynamics built 894 upgraded M1s called the Improved Product M1 (IPM1). The IPM1 retained the same M68E1 105mm rifled main gun as the M1.

The IPM1 was an interim vehicle version with various improvements to accommodate the up-gunned M1A1 version to follow. The IPM1 included a beefed-up suspension system with increased-capacity shock absorbers. Improvements were also made to the vehicle's transmission, armor protection, and main gun mount. This boosted the vehicle weight to about 61 tons.

The M1s and IPM1s were withdrawn from active Army service by 1995. They were then passed to the Army's Reserves and National Guard tank units, while others were retained for possible rebuilding into newer versions of the M1 series. Some were intended for conversion into bridge launchers, armored recovery vehicles (ARVs), and other support vehicles.

Due to funding constraints, only 44 Abrams-based bridge-launchers, officially nicknamed Wolverines, were built by GDLS for the Army. To make up for the shortfall of Wolverines, the Army plans to upgrade its existing inventory of M60-series tank-based bridge launchers.

A U.S. Marine Corps M1A1 tank armed with a smooth-bore 120mm main gun comes off a southern California beach. The M1A1 was acquired by the Corps to replace its aging inventory of M60A1 tanks that first entered service in 1977. *Greg Stewart*

M1A1 Abrams

The third version of the Abrams was the M1A1, an M1 with Block I Product Improvements. Production of the M1A1 began in August 1985 and continued in the United States until 1993. General Dynamics Land System (GDLS) built 4,550 new M1A1s, which made it the most numerous version of the Abrams tank in the Army's inventory. In addition, GDLS built 269 M1A1s for the Marine Corps in 1991. The Marine Corps refers to them as the M1A1 Common tank because they have a number of features such as more tie-down points and provisions for a Deep Water Fording Kit (DWFK) not seen on M1A1 tanks before

1991. All Army M1A1 tanks built after 1991 have these features. In 1994 and 1995 Congress provided funding to transfer 134 Army M1A1s to the Marine Corps inventory. They consisted of 84 pre-1991 M1A1 tanks and 48 Army examples of the M1A1 Common tank. In early 2003 the Army decided to transfer 12 additional M1A1 Common Tanks to the Marine Corps Inventory.

The major design change for the new M1A1 was the inclusion of a 120mm smoothbore main gun designated M256. The weapon is an American-built version of a German tank gun design. Whereas twisted lands and grooves inside a rifled gun barrel spin the projectiles to stabilize them in flight, the M256 gun bore is smooth to accommodate modern projectiles that are stabilized in flight by small fins. Smoothbore tank guns have big advantages for the Army since they are cheaper to build than rifled tank guns and do not wear out as quickly. For the same explosive charge, the muzzle velocity of a smoothbore gun is higher because the energy that would have been required to rotate the projectile goes into the velocity.

Like the rifled 105mm main gun in the earlier version of the Abrams, the 120mm gun in the M1A1 is fully stabilized in azimuth and elevation. This feature provides high target accuracy while the vehicle is in motion, even on moderately rough terrain. It is also equipped, like the older 105mm gun, with a fume evacuator, and a thermal shroud and muzzle-reference sensor to compensate for gun warp. As any gun barrel heats or cools, its aim point changes. Firing, weather, and gravity all have an effect on the barrel and its aim.

As expected, the larger gun has superior range and penetration capabilities compared to the 105mm rifled main gun mounted on the M1 and IPM1. During America's first war with Iraq in 1991, M1A1s effectively engaged enemy targets at ranges of over 2 miles with their 120mm main guns.

One drawback is the larger diameter of the gun's ammunition. Compared to the 55 rounds of 105mm main gun ammunition carried in the M1 and IPM1, the M1A1 can carry only 40 main gun rounds—34 in the rear turret bustle and 6 in an armored box in the hull. This disadvantage is offset by the improved accuracy of the gun. A new digital fire-control computer in the M1A1 tank is an improved version of the computer in the M1 and IPM1 tanks. The combination of the very accurate fire-control computer and higher lethality of the 120mm rounds enables the M1A1 tank to

An M1A1 tank fires its 120mm main gun at a pop-up target located about a mile and a half down range at the U.S. Army's National Training Center, located in southern California. The bright streak of the tracer element of the main gun round comes out of the fireball. *Greg Stewart*

A young Marine Corps tanker on the outside of an M1A1 tank turret carefully holds an armor-piercing, fin-stabilized, discarding sabot, tracer (APFSDS-T) main gun target practice (TP) round. The tanker will hand the round to the tank's loader inside the vehicle through the overhead hatch in the turret. *Greg Stewart*

destroy an enemy target with fewer rounds than it took with the M1 or IPM1 tanks.

Along with the new German-designed 120mm main gun and the upgraded fire-control computer system, the M1A1 received better armor protection and an overpressure system designed to keep nuclear-, biological-, or chemical-contaminated air out of the crew compartment. The new main gun and thicker armor increased the weight of the most recent version to about 68 tons. This extra weight forced GDLS to make improvements to the vehicle's suspension, transmission, and final drives.

Main Gun Ammunition
The current main tank-killing round for the M1A1's 120mm main gun is the M829A2 armor-piercing,

This photograph was taken inside the turret of a Marine Corps M1A1 tank and shows the storage arrangement of 16 of the 34 120mm main gun rounds stored in the vehicle's rear turret bustle. The main gun rounds are located directly behind the loader's position and can be removed without the loader leaving his or her seat. *Greg Stewart*

fin-stabilized, discarding sabot, tracer round (APFSDS-T). It is about 3 feet long and weighs about 50 pounds. A 6-pound penetrating metal dart made out of depleted uranium (DU) shoots out of the barrel at incredibly high speed. It can punch a hole through the thickest tank armor. The M829A2 is described in military terms as a kinetic energy (KE) round.

Because the diameter of the DU penetrating dart is much smaller than the caliber of the 120mm main gun on the M1A1, the dart is centered in a larger-diameter carrier called a sabot. The lightweight sabot carrier falls off shortly after the DU penetrating dart leaves the barrel of a tank's main gun.

Another very potent tank-killing round that can be fired from the 120mm main gun on the M1A1 is the M830A1 high-explosive antitank-tracer (HEAT-T). Unlike the M829A2 KE round that uses brute strength to penetrate armor, the M830A1 round has a shaped-charge (chemical energy) warhead that explodes on impact. A shaped-charge warhead is designed to direct explosive forces in a single direction

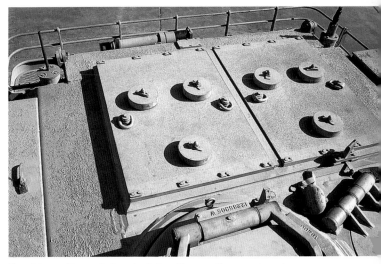

Two blow-off panels located directly over the rear turret bustle of a Marine Corps M1A1 are visible in this photograph. If the propellants contained within the stored main-gun rounds explode, the force is vented upward through the blow-off panels. *Greg Stewart*

with a configuration designed to defeat a particular armor design. Most of the energy of that explosion is forced against the target in a high-speed jet stream. This jet of hot gasses penetrates armor and causes interior destruction due to the heat of the gases, blast, and fragmentation of the projectile and armor. Besides killing tanks, the M830A1 is also very effective against bunkers or lightly or non-armored vehicles.

A new antipersonnel canister round for the 120mm main gun on the M1A1 began operational testing in 2003. This round, the XM1028, has a payload of 900 to 1,000 tungsten spheres that will leave the barrel of the M1A1 main gun at high velocity in a shotgun-like pattern. U.S. Army and Marine Corps M48A3 Patton tank crews effectively used canister rounds against enemy infantry formations during the Vietnam War.

M1A1 HA Abrams: Armor Upgrades

The Chobham armor fitted to the turret and hull of the first M1s and early M1A1s was unsurpassed in its ability to defeat shaped-charge warheads. However, it was penetrated by newer generations of kinetic energy (KE) armor-piercing rounds that began to appear in the 1980s.

For protection against KE rounds, an important armor upgrade was made to all M1A1s that came off the GDLS production line beginning in May 1988. Depleted uranium armor (DU) was added to the armor recipe at the front of the turret. The DU armor added an extra ton of weight to the M1A1. According to the Army and GDLS, export versions of the Abrams do not contain DU armor. They do, however, have another very effective armor package installed.

M1A1s equipped with the improved armor protection are designated M1A1 HA (heavy armor) tanks. There are no visible differences between a standard

A U.S. Army M1A1 tank is pictured in a German field during a 1988 training exercise. An important external spotting feature of the M1A1 tank is the large hump-shaped bore evacuator located in the middle of the barrel. The bore evacuator on the M1 and IPM1 tanks is smaller and more evenly rounded. *Michael Green*

A U.S. Marine Corps M1A1 tank is guided onto a U.S. Navy Landing Craft, Air Cushioned (LCAC). A plated-over circular fitting that designates the vehicle as a late-production M1A1 is in front of the loader's overhead hatch position. The opening was for the possible addition of a second thermal sight at a later date. *Greg Stewart*

M1A1 and the M1A1 HA model. The crews of heavy armor M1A1s enjoyed an unparalleled level of protection during Operation Desert Storm. American M1A1 HA tanks took point-blank hits from Iraqi 125mm T72 tank main guns with no more damage than a dent.

The armor design on all versions of the M1 Abrams tank series concentrates on threats to its front. However, in urban combat, a threat can come from any direction, including overhead. The U.S. Army Armor Center is considering a number of different add-on armor kits to protect vulnerable areas of the

vehicle, such as the top of the turret and the rear hull engine deck. Redesigned armored engine grilles for the MIAI tanks were sent to Iraq during Operation Iraqi Freedom.

Additional Upgrades: MIAI D Abrams

Despite the end of the M1A1 production in 1993, the Army continued to improve the vehicle's combat effectiveness. A major upgrade was the incorporation of information-age technology. The result was the deployment in 2000 of the first two battalions (95

An M1A1 tank with a mine plough at the front of the vehicle's hull is pictured at the U.S. Army's National Training Center (NTC). When lowered into the ground, this 4.5-ton device can clear mines buried in front of the vehicle's path up to a depth of 2 to 4 inches in front of each track. It is based on a Soviet Army design. *Greg Stewart*

vehicles) of a new variant of the M1A1, unofficially designated the M1A1 D ("D" for "digitized"). There are no external differences between the M1A1 D and other versions of the M1A1.

The M1A1 D is equipped with an add-on computer with a keyboard and monitor screen installed at the vehicle commander's position. The Army calls this computer hardware and its software the Force 21 Battle Command Brigade-and-Below (FBCB2) system. The primary function of the FBCB2 system is to send and receive automatic position location reports from its interface with the Global Positioning System (GPS). It also sends and receives command-and-control graphic or text message traffic via a wireless tactical internet routed through secure digital radio transmissions.

Once the M1A1 D vehicle commander logs onto the FBCB2 system, the monitor screen will display a constantly updated computer-generated digital map to show with blue icons the position of all friendly units that have the same FBCB2 system. The area

Next page: Based on the chassis of an upgraded M1 tank, the M104 Wolverine can carry, launch, and recover a 12-ton portable bridge that can cover a gap of almost 80 feet when fully extended. The portable bridge is able to support a 70-ton moving vehicle. *General Dynamic*

23

Marine Corps tankers clean the air filters (called V-Packs) on the rear hull of their M1A1 tank. Turbine engines require more filtered air for combustion than comparable diesel engines. Later models of the Abrams tank have self-cleaning air filters. *Greg Stewart*

encompassed by the digital map display can extend for many miles in every direction. The same information also appears on every other computer monitor screen within the FBCB2 network. At the Army Brigade level, this may encompass up to 1,000 computers. Command and control has become much easier at all levels, since commanders know precisely where all their forces are at any given time.

The FBCB2 will display enemy units as red icons. The information on the location of enemy units is provided by a variety of sensors mounted on ground and aerial platforms located on and around the battlefield area. The sensor platforms themselves can be manned or unmanned systems.

The ability of M1A1 D tank commanders and the command personnel all the way up to brigade level to "see" the location of all their and the enemy's vehicles on computer-generated digital maps provides them with situational awareness. In the simplest of terms, situational awareness means the M1A1 D tank commanders and their superiors will be able to choose a course of action before their enemy counterparts are even aware of their presence on the battlefield. They may organize an ambush of an advancing enemy formation at a favorable location, or call upon supporting assets such as field artillery or helicopter gunships to increase the odds in their favor before they begin their own attack, if even needed.

An M1A2 tank takes part in a training exercise at the Army's NTC. The major identification feature of the vehicle is the addition of the periscope-like head of the commander's independent thermal viewer (CITV), located directly in front of the loader's overhead hatch position. *Greg Stewart*

The Army's M1A1s have been heavily used in both combat and training. Like all machines, they become less reliable over time. Instead of building new ones, the Army is rebuilding 790 older model M1A1s from the ground up. The rebuilt tanks will be in like-new condition when completed. The rebuild project started in 1999 and is called the Abrams Integrated Management (AIM) overhaul program. It will take until 2008 to run all the vehicles through the AIM program. An important part of the AIM program will be updating the vehicles into the D model with the add-on FBCB2 system if funding is available.

This is a close-up photograph of the fixed tank commander's weapon cupola on a U.S. Army M1A2 tank. On the M1A1 tank, the vehicle commander turned his cupola to fire the .50-caliber (12.7mm) machine gun. On the M1A2, the machine gun is attached to a ring that rotates around the fixed cupola. *Greg Stewart*

M1A2 Abrams

The fourth version of the Abrams is the M1A2, or M1 with Block II Product Improvements. (The M1A1 D is not recognized as a separate version of the Abrams series.) General Dynamics Land System was awarded the contract for full-scale development of the M1A2 version of the Abrams in December 1988. The GLDS delivered the first five prototypes of the M1A2 to the Army in March 1992. The Army was very impressed with the results and quickly approved low-rate production of 62 new M1A2 tanks that same month. The first of these vehicles were turned over to the Army in November 1992, and the last arrived in April 1993.

Instead of building more new M1A2 tanks, the Army decided to have GDLS upgrade early-model M1 tanks to the M1A2 standard. In September 1994, a contract was awarded to GDLS to convert 206 M1 tanks into M1A2 tanks. These vehicles were delivered

to the Army between October 1994 and September 1996. A follow-on contract was awarded to GDLS in 1996 for the conversion of 580 additional M1 tanks to the M1A2 standard. The Army also picked up an option for another 20 M1s to be upgraded to the M1A2 standard. Thus, GDLS was committed to deliver a total of 600 M1 tanks upgraded to the M1A2 standard to the Army by July 2001. However, the Army revised its contract with GDLS in February 1999 so the last 240 M1 tanks to be upgraded to the M1A2 standard would be upgraded to an even more advanced configuration called the M1A2 SEP (systems enhancements package). Because of the revised contract, a total of only 360 M1 tanks were upgraded to the M1A2 standard by GDLS in its second contract with the Army. There were a total of 628 M1A2 tanks built. At the present time, 247 M1A2s are in storage with no plans to reissue them to any units.

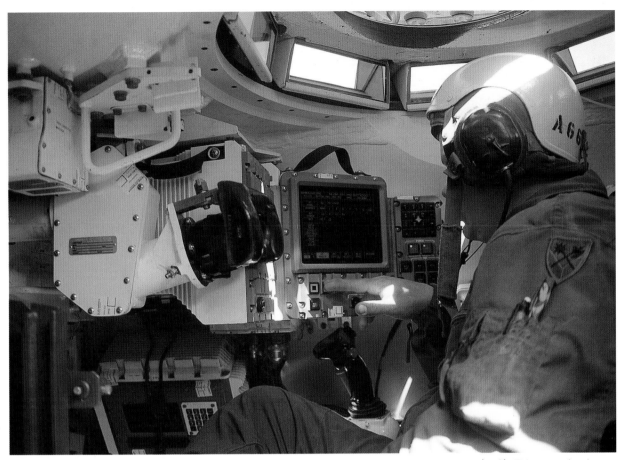

A vehicle commander in an M1A2 tank inputs data into his inter-vehicular information system (IVIS). This now obsolete computer-based system indicates where the tank is located on the ground, where friendly forces are in relation to it, and where enemy forces have been identified. The information is projected on a monochrome monitor screen. *Greg Stewart*

As with the M1A1 HA version, the M1A2 has DU armor incorporated into its composite armor on the front of its turret. The DU armor in the M1A2 is even better than the armor in the HA variant and offers protection from all present KE antitank rounds and even those that will be created within the next decade. The addition of more DU armor to the M1A2, along with a host of other improvements, has raised the weight of the M1A2 up to 68.4 tons.

The M1A2 retained the M256 120mm main gun from the MA1. However, the ammunition racks in the M1A2 turret bustle were redesigned to store two additional main gun rounds within the tank. This gives the M1A2 a main gun ammunition load of 42 rounds.

The major visible difference between the various versions of the M1A1 and the M1A2 is the addition of the large periscope-like head of the commander's independent thermal viewer (CITV). It is located on the top of the vehicle's turret in front of the loader's hatch. The addition of the CITV on the M1A2 provides the vehicle crew access to a second thermal sight in addition to the single gunner's thermal imaging system (TIS) sight found on all the earlier versions of the Abrams series.

The gunner's TIS forms an important part of what is called the gunner's primary sight (GPS). The GPS is the gunner's main optical sighting instrument and includes a laser range finder. The vehicle commander has an extension to the GPS in all the various versions of the Abrams series, so he can see what the gunner is looking at. The upper portion of the GPS is located on the turret roof of all Abrams series tanks in front of the vehicle commander's cupola and is protected by a steel armor box. Small armored doors swing outward when the sight is in use.

The CITV, serving as a second thermal viewer in the M1A2, gives the vehicle commander a 360-degree, all-weather, day-night view of the battlefield that he can operate independently of the gunner's thermal sighting system. This allows the commander and gunner to act as a "hunter-killer" team. The vehicle commander can search for new targets while the gunner engages the current target in his field of view. After the M1A2 gunner fires the tank's main gun, the vehicle commander "hands-off" a new target to the gunner with the push of a designate button. The turret immediately rotates to face the new target selected by the vehicle commander. This feature allows M1A2 crews to engage multiple targets about 40 percent faster than M1A1 crews.

Another key difference between the M1A2 and its predecessors is the incorporation of digital electronics and microprocessor controls. Electronics technology has greatly improved the reliability and operational capability of the M1A2 compared to earlier versions in the series.

The M1A2, which was designed in 1988, possessed enough on-board data processing capability that it did not require the same add-on computer hardware as was later incorporated into the M1A1 D. Like the M1A1 D, M1A2 has a keyboard and a monochrome monitor screen capable of displaying to the

An M1A2 tank races into action at the Army's NTC. The introduction of this vehicle into Army service was revolutionary at the time due to the incorporation of commercial-based information-age technology into the design. *Greg Stewart*

commander digital maps and text, providing almost the same level of situational awareness as the M1A1 D. Unfortunately, the command-and-control computer hardware and software of the M1A2, the inter-vehicular information system (IVIS), is no longer compatible with the newer FBCB2 system in the M1A1 D and the M1A2 SEP tanks.

M1A2 SEP Abrams

The developmental history of the M1A2 systems enhancements package (SEP) tank can be traced back to early 1994, when the Army identified several important upgrades it wanted to add to the basic

M1A2 tank. Rather than wait for GDLS to convert 600 M1 tanks to the basic M1A2 configuration by 2001, the Army revised that contract to have the last 240 M1 tanks upgraded to the M1A2 SEP standard rather than just the M1A2 standard. This was followed by another Army contract awarded to GDLS in April 2001 to upgrade 307 additional M1 tanks to the M1A2 SEP standard. This process began in August 2001 and will be completed by the end of 2004. In addition, the Army awarded GDLS a smaller contract to upgrade 41 basic M1A2 tanks to the M1A2 SEP standard by 2004. When all the contracts are completed by GDLS, the Army will have a total of 588 M1A2 SEP tanks in service.

A vehicle commander of an M1A2 SEP tank looks at his commander's display unit (CDU). It consists of two monitor screens. The upper screen projects an electronic image generated by the commander's independent thermal viewer (CITV). *Hans Halberstadt*

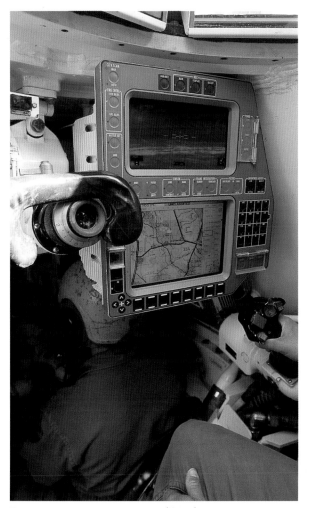

The commander's display unit (CDU) that is located inside an M1A2 SEP tank turret. The bottom monitor projects a constantly updated digitized color map that shows terrain features with grids and displays a vehicle's location, the location of friendly units, and any known enemy forces. *Hans Halberstadt*

There are no major external differences between the M1A2 SEP and the original M1A2 tank, except for an armored box located in the rear turret bustle of the M1A2 SEP that contains the vehicle's thermal management system (TMS). A key element of the M1A2 SEP project is the upgrade of the vehicle's hardware and software with the latest commercial electronic developments. A TMS has also been added to the M1A2 SEP. The system is designed to keep the temperature within the crew compartment under 95 degrees no matter how hot or humid it may be outside the vehicle. Holding temperatures to moderate levels has obvious benefits for crew effectiveness, but the major reason is to improve the reliability of the electronic equipment. The interior of a combat vehicle in extreme heat can reach temperatures that will not allow the electronics to cool adequately. Although the electronics in the M1A2 and M1A2 SEP are designed to withstand extreme temperatures under severe conditions, the reliability of the electronic systems can be reduced and computer performance can be impacted. The increased computer capability of the M1A2 SEP compared to the M1A2 resulted in higher heat generation and drove the need for the TMS system.

Another important M1A2 SEP technology upgrade is the second-generation forward-looking infrared radar (FLIR) sight (SGF). The SGF sight provides the M1A2 SEP vehicle commander and gunner with a 70 percent improvement in accuracy over the original M1A2 sight.

The SGF has different magnification positions for targets at various ranges. The three- and six-power positions provide a very wide field of view for close targets. The 13- and 25-power positions are used for intermediate-range targets. A 50-power position gives the M1A2 crew the ability to discern and positively identify targets at extreme long ranges to lessen the chances of fratricide in battle.

For roughly the next two decades, the cutting edge of the Army's ground power will consist of its 588 M1A2 SEP tanks. The last will be delivered in 2004. These M1A2 SEP tanks will be supported by almost 800 M1A1 tanks rebuilt under the AIM program. That program is slated for completion by 2008. This inventory of almost 1,400 M1 Abrams-series tanks is and will be divided among the active Army's five heavy divisions. The M1A2 SEP tanks are currently concentrated in the Fourth Infantry Division (formerly the Second Armored Division) and the First Cavalry Division. Both divisions are based at Fort Hood, Texas, and form part of the III Corps.

ARMORED INFANTRY VEHICLES

In late 1944, the Army began design studies for a fully tracked armored infantry vehicle with an armored roof. The Army's efforts did not come to fruition until 1950, when the steel-hull M75 armored infantry vehicle rolled off the production lines.

The M75 was quickly followed by the steel-hull M59. At this point, the Army called these vehicles armored personnel carriers (APCs) instead of armored infantry vehicles. The Army fielded 6,300 M59 APCs between 1953 and 1960. Unfortunately, the M59's powertrain was unreliable and lacked an adequate operational range. The Army looked for a suitable replacement vehicle that weighed less than the M59 and was more affordable.

M113 Armored Personnel Carrier

The Food Machinery Corporation (FMC) solved the multiple-design problems to reduce weight and cost and still provide effective armor protection and mobility. The development of lightweight aluminum armor alloys and the technology to weld large plates together formed the basis for the low-cost and effective troop transport known as the M113 APC. With an industrial gasoline engine and commercial transmission in the first M113s, FMC furnished an APC that cost about the same as luxury cars of the era.

The first production M113 APCs came off the assembly line in 1960. M113s have a two-person crew: a driver and vehicle commander. The driver's station is at the front left corner of the hull, and the engine compartment is to the right of the driver. The vehicle commander's station is in the center of the vehicle. There is additional space for an 11-man infantry squad.

A U.S. Army M113A1 from a headquarters unit takes part in a training exercise at the U.S. Army's NTC sometime in the late 1980s. An M2HB .50-caliber (12.7mm) machine gun, the standard armament for most versions of the M113 series, is mounted on the vehicle commander's cupola. *Greg Stewart*

CHAPTER 2

There are no provisions for the squad to fire weapons from within the vehicle. Rather, the squad engages enemy forces on foot after leaving the vehicle through the large power-operated rear ramp. The M113 vehicle commander can provide supporting fire with the .50-caliber M2HB Browning machine gun mounted on the cupola. The M113's aluminum alloy armor provided protection only from some types of small arms fire and artillery fragments.

The upgraded M113A1 began production in 1964. The gasoline engine was replaced by a 212-horsepower diesel engine. The U.S. Army received about 5,000 M113A1s between 1964 and 1979. A total of 23,576 were built.

Even before M113A1 production ended, the Army planned to create the M113A2. The M113A2 was successful enough to warrant the Army's initiating a product improvement program (PIP) to upgrade a large portion of its M113 and M113A1 inventory. The Army also ordered 2,660 brand-new M113A2s from FMC. Production for the M113A2s started in 1979.

The M113A2 retained the same highly reliable and extremely durable powertrain as the M113A1, but improvements were made to the cooling system to increase its efficiency and reduce the build up of debris. Major improvements in torsion bar metallurgy made it possible to increase road wheel travel by 50 percent. This increased cross-country speed to 30 miles per hour.

In the late 1980s, the M113A3 was another major product improvement. The engine was turbocharged, power was increased to 275 horsepower, and the cooling system was improved. A major improvement in survivability was from spall liners in the sides, roof, and rear of the troop compartment of the M113A3. These liners capture fragments of the aluminum hull that could become interior projectiles if the hull is struck or penetrated by a projectile.

A squad of U.S. Army infantrymen disembarks from an M113A1 armored personnel carrier (APC). The large ramp at the rear of the vehicle's hull, common to all M113-series vehicles, is operated by hydraulics and contains a door to use when the ramp is closed. *United Defense*

An M113A2 APC of the California National Guard comes off a portable bridge during a training exercise in the summer of 1985. A distinguishing feature of the M113A2 is the smoke grenade launchers on either side of the front hull below the headlights. *Michael Green*

The addition of two external fuel tanks at the rear of the vehicle was another major improvement. This freed up 16 cubic feet of under-armor volume for additional stowage. Fuel capacity remained unchanged at 95 gallons. The external fuel tanks also give an added margin of protection from fuel-generated fires or explosions. The two rear-mounted external fuel tanks are the most easily observed exterior characteristics of the M113A3 that distinguishs it from its predecessors.

At the beginning of 2003, the Army had 14,975 M113-series vehicles in 16 different variants. Models also exist to deliver smoke (two variants), transport engineer squads, evacuate wounded, provide mortar support, designate targets, command and control (two variants), transport infantry, and conduct training (modified to look like enemy vehicles). Roughly 6,000 vehicles of the M113 series are M113A3s. This number includes 500 brand-new M113A3 vehicles produced for the Army by United Defense LP (UDLP) Ground Systems Division (formerly FMC) between 1987 and 1992. The remainder consists of M113A2s. There are no M113s or M113A1s in Army service. All of these have been upgraded or scrapped.

During upgrade activities conducted in a partnership with Anniston Army Depot, several new modifications were added, including NBC equipment and a passive night vision device for the driver. A new track, the T-150, is being added to increase track life by four times. The Army plans to equip a portion of its M113A3 fleet with digital command and control systems comparable with those of the M1A1 D and M1A2 SEP Abrams tanks. These upgrades will allow the M113A3 to operate effectively alongside the Army's other weapon platforms. The M113A2s and M113A3s are part of the Army's Legacy Force.

Bradley Fighting Vehicles

In the early 1960s, the Army needed a tracked armored vehicle that allowed onboard infantry to fire their weapons from within the safety of the vehicle. This weapon system would also be armed with a turret-operated weapon system that could destroy lightly armored enemy vehicles. Another important requirement was automotive performance comparable with the next generation of highly mobile Army tanks that would replace the M60 series.

Many companies were interested in the opportunity to develop a new armored infantry vehicle for the

An M113A2 is recognizable by the smoke grenade launcher brackets on the front hull. The M113A2, like its predecessors, was about 16 feet long; 8 feet, 10 inches wide; and 8 feet, 2 inches high with the vehicle's commander's machine gun fitted. *Michael Green*

An M113A3 stops on a country road in Germany. The vehicle belongs to a U.S. Army engineering unit, which is evident by the rolls of barbed wire on the trailer being towed behind. A distinguishing feature of the M113A3 is the thicker buoyancy trim vane on the front of the vehicle's hull. *Michael Green*

Army. However, FMC, the designer of the highly successful M113, was awarded a contract in November 1972 to develop what the Army referred to as the XM723 Mechanized Infantry Combat Vehicle (MICV). Besides carrying a nine-member infantry squad, the XM723 was armed with a 20mm automatic cannon fitted in a one-person turret. Fiscal limits imposed by Congress forced the Army to merge the MICV program in 1976 with a recently cancelled program called the Armored Reconnaissance Scout Vehicle (ARSV). The MICV would be configured to serve as

an infantry squad vehicle or reconnaissance vehicle. To fulfill the cavalry's need for a tank-killing weapon, the Army decided the MICV required a larger two-man turret equipped with an antitank missile launcher device.

Reflecting the many changes to the design of the MICV and its two different battlefield roles, the Army assigned the vehicle two different designations: the XM2 Infantry Fighting Vehicle (IFV) and the XM3 Cavalry Fighting Vehicle (CFV). (The "X" stands for experimental and is dropped from a vehicle's designation after

Another distinguishing feature of the M113A3 is the two external fuel tanks at the rear of the vehicle's hull. This particular M113A3 is also fitted with the P900 appliqué armor hull kit and armor gun shield kit for the vehicle commander's position. The U.S. Army did not adopt the optional P900 armored kit offered by the manufacturer. The Army still employs its Vietnam War-era armor gun shield kits on many of its existing fleet of M113-series vehicles. *United Defense*

it is placed into series production.) Production versions of both vehicles entered Army service in 1981 and were nicknamed Bradley in honor of General Omar N. Bradley. He was the commander of all U.S. Army forces in Western Europe during the last two years of World War II and served as the Chief of Staff of the Army after the war.

All the various versions of the M2 IFV and M3 CFV have a large two-man armored turret armed with a high-velocity M242 25mm chain gun, an automatic cannon effective against lightly armored enemy vehicles and slow- and low-flying aerial targets such as helicopters. A coaxial M240 7.62mm machine gun is mounted alongside the 25mm automatic cannon. The size of the turret basket within the vehicle's hull limits the troop complement to no more than seven infantry members in the various versions of the M2 IFV. Periscopes and firing ports on the sides and rear of the early versions of the M2 IFV hull allow the infantry members to fight from within the confines of their vehicle. They embark or disembark through a large, power-operated rear ramp.

The business end of an M2A1 Bradley Infantry Fighting Vehicle (IFV). Visible in this photograph taken at Camp Roberts, California, is the vehicle's two-person, all-electric stabilized turret armed with a 25mm automatic cannon, coaxial 7.62mm machine gun, and an antitank missile launcher unit. The large flat plate on the front of the hull is the trim vane. *Michael Green*

All versions of the M3 CFV carry a complement of two scouts in the rear hull compartment. The extra room not occupied by passengers is configured to carry more ammunition and additional antitank missiles. All the various versions of the M2 IFV and the M3 CFV form part of the Bradley Fighting Vehicle (BFV) family of vehicles.

All the various versions of the M2 IFV and M3 CFV are fitted with a launcher to fire tube-launched, optically tracked, wire-command link-guided (TOW) antitank missiles. The armored launcher itself contains two of the ready-to-fire roughly 50-pound TOW

missiles. Viewed from the front, the missile launcher is stowed vertically against the right side of the turret when not in use. When it's ready to fire, the TOW launcher is raised to a horizontal position. The gunner then aims and fires a missile and uses the integrated sight unit (ISU) to steer the missile to its target. The ISU contains both a daylight sight and a thermal imaging sight.

To keep up with the Army's M1 Abrams tanks, the early versions of the M2 IFV and M3 CFV were fitted with a front-mounted Cummins 500-horsepower VTA turbocharged diesel engine. It provided the

This M2A1 Bradley took part in a large-scale training exercise conducted in West Germany in 1988. The 25mm automatic cannon in the vehicle's turret can fire single shots or at selectable rates of fire of 100 or 200 rounds per minute. It fires both armor-piercing discarding sabot (APDS) rounds or high-explosive incendiary (HEI) rounds. *Michael Green*

power for rapid acceleration, agile steering, and sustained high speed both on- and off-road. The vehicles have a top road speed of about 40 miles per hour.

The turrets and hulls of all the various versions of the M2 IFV and M3 CFV are constructed of aluminum alloy armor. Additional ballistic protection is provided by steel spaced laminate armor on the hull and turret of the M2 IFV, M3 CFV, M2A1 IFV, and M3A1 CFV. This form of armor protection can stop 14.5mm armor-piercing machine-gun rounds and 152mm artillery air-burst and ground-burst fragments.

The original M2 IFVs and M3 CFVs are no longer in active Army service. FMC built 2,300 examples of the original version of the Bradley vehicles, also called the basic or A0 model, and another 1,371 examples of the A1 versions. Some Army National Guard units still have the original A0 and A1 Bradley vehicles in service. The biggest improvement to the A1 version of the Bradley over the original A0 version was the modified armored missile launchers. The launchers could now fire the TOW II, a more powerful version of the TOW antitank missile.

An M2A1 Bradley IFV fords a small stream. The 25mm automatic cannon in the vehicle's turret can be employed to destroy lightly armored vehicles and antitank emplacements. The coaxial M240 7.62mm machine gun is used to engage dismounted infantry, crew-served weapons, antitank guided missile teams, and unarmored wheeled or tracked vehicles. *Michael Green*

In the early 1980s, there was a great deal of media attention given to a perceived weakness in the Bradley's armor protection. In response to public opinion, Congressional involvement, and a new up-armed Soviet IFV (the BMP-2) equipped with a 30mm automatic cannon, the Army increased the Bradley's armor protection. The Block II upgrades went into production in 1988. The upgraded vehicles were designated M2A2 and M3A2.

The A2 steel appliqué (bolt-on) armor on the hull and turret was designed to stop 30mm armor-piercing ammunition and 152mm artillery air bursts. This change eliminated the firing ports, which were viewed as a weakness in the overall armor protection of the A0 and A1 versions of the Bradley.

The A2 armor design included attachment points for extra protection in the form of passive armor or explosive reactive armor tiles. The vehicles were also fitted with spall liners. To compensate for the significant added weight of the new armor package, engine power was raised to 600 horsepower. The A2 versions of the Bradley weighed about 30 tons.

The A2 versions are called the High Survivability Bradley vehicles. By the time A2 production ended in 1994, FMC had built 4,641 Bradley IFVs and 2,083 CFVs, for a total of 6,724 vehicles.

Combat experience gained during Operation Desert Storm in 1991 resulted in several modifications, including a Global Positioning System (GPS) and a laser range finder. An antitank missile countermeasure

The A2 versions of the Bradley Fighting Vehicles (BFVs) have no trim vane on their front hulls, as seen in this photo of an M2A2 IFV. To retain their amphibious abilities, the A2 versions of the BFVs have a flotation or water barrier stowed around the periphery of the vehicle's hull. *Michael Green*

A distinguishing feature of the A2 version of the BFVs is the large, flat steel armor panels that cover both sides of the hull. This M2A2 IFV is operating at high speed. Loaded for combat, the A2 versions of the BFVs can accelerate from a standing start to 30 miles per hour in less than 22 seconds. *Michael Green*

device was also attached to the top of the turret. The upgraded vehicles are called the M2A2 and M3A2 Operation Desert Storm (ODS) Bradleys. The Army upgraded 1,423 A2s to the ODS standard between 1999 and 2000.

The newest Bradley upgrades, the M2A3 IFV and the M3A3 CFV, were delivered to the Army in 2000. The Army upgraded 1,602 A2 vehicles to the A3 standard. The A3 upgrade program is scheduled for completion in 2004. In February 2003, the Army decided to divert funding from the Bradley A3 upgrade program to the upcoming Objective Force. Hence, the total number of A3 BFVs to enter in the Army service will be limited to about half the original number envisioned.

The most important A3 upgrade is the addition of a digital FBCB2 command and control system comparable to that in the M1A1 D and M1A2 SEP Abrams tanks. This gives Bradleys the ability to join the new digital battlefield network. Like the M113s, Bradley vehicles are a large part of the Army's Legacy Force.

The distinguishing visible feature on the new, digitized A3 Bradleys is the second-generation forward-looking infrared radar (FLIR) mounted on the left rear of the turret. It is called the commander's independent viewer (CIV) and can be rotated 360 degrees without moving the vehicle's turret. The CIV allows the Bradley vehicle commander to identify targets up to four miles away in darkness or poor weather conditions while the gunner engages another target with his own thermal sight. Like the hunter-killer system on the M1A2 and M1A2 SEP tanks, the A3 Bradley commander can push a designate button that will automatically move the vehicle's turret in the direction of a new target immediately after the gunner has fired on the target in his or her sight picture.

Before the A3 upgrades, the gunner or commander had to estimate range to the target. Zeroing in usually required a few trial shots before the target was hit. The new laser range finder instantly determines target range and uses that information to accurately point the gun. This almost guarantees a first-shot hit.

Other A3 improvements include better top armor. This change reflects the growing number of top-attack weapons used by enemy armies. There is

also an upgraded chemical protection system that will provide decontaminated air to occupants when the vehicle is exposed to chemical or biological agents. The system will also allow A3 Bradley vehicles to operate in areas of nuclear contamination.

The two Bradley fighting vehicle variants currently in Army service consists of the M6 Bradley Linebacker air-defense system and the M7 Bradley Fire Support Vehicle (BFIST). Both are based on the M2A2 IFV chassis and look very similar with a large armored box attached to the right side of the turret.

The Bradley Linebacker's armored launcher on the right side of the turret contains four Stinger ground-to-air antiaircraft missiles. An additional six Stinger reload missiles are carried onboard. The armored box on the M7 BFIST contains a laser range finder and various day/night optical sights.

The A2 versions of the BFVs were designed with attachment points to mount explosive reactive armor tiles. A U.S. Army M2A2 Bradley IFV pictured in Somalia in November 1993 is fitted with its full set of reactive armor tiles on both its hull and turret. *DVIC*

The M7 BFIST is used to control indirect artillery and mortar fire on the battlefield in support of the Army's frontline Legacy Force vehicles. It first entered Army service in 2000 and will supplement the Army's existing inventory of Fire Support Team Vehicles (FISTV) based on the chassis of the M113 series vehicles. The total production run of M7 Bradley vehicles will consist of just over 100 examples. Plans are being made to create a more advanced digitized version of the BFIST based on the M2A3 chassis.

Stryker Infantry Carrier Vehicle (ICV)

The Army took a historical step in early 2000 when it ordered its first all-wheeled armored personnel carrier. The 19-ton, eight-wheeled vehicle is made from high-hardness steel alloy armor and called the Infantry Carrier Vehicle (ICV). It is powered by a 350-horsepower Caterpillar diesel engine that gives it a top road speed of 60 miles per hour. The ICV crew consists of a vehicle commander and driver. In the rear hull compartment of the ICV, a nine-member infantry squad can be carried in reasonable comfort. There are no provisions for the squad members to fire their individual weapons from within the hull. With its fuel tanks topped off, the ICV has a useful range of about 400 miles on flat roads.

The eight large tires of the ICV have run-flat capability and are connected to a central tire inflation system that allows the driver to adjust air pressure to match the terrain. The Air Force's C-130 Hercules transport plane can carry a single ICV, and the newer and larger C-17 Globemaster III can carry three ICVs at a time. The C-5A Galaxy can carry five ICVs at a time.

Armament on the ICV consists of a Remote Weapon Station (RWS) mount of either a .50-caliber M2HB machine gun or a Mk. 19 40mm automatic

Top: An important feature of the A3 version of the BFV is the commander's independent viewer (CIV), seen in this photo on the left side of the turret roof. It rotates 360 degrees and allows the vehicle commander to search independently from his gunner for targets on the battlefield, day or night. *United Defense*

Left: The troop compartment of an M2A3 IFV. Bench seats for the infantry squad members are on either side of the hull compartment. The vehicle's circular turret basket, which is occupied by the vehicle commander and gunner, is at the far end. *Hans Halberstadt*

The armored pod that contains the Bradley Linebacker's ready-to-fire Stinger missiles is located on the right side of the vehicle's turret, as seen in this photo. The Stingers are equally effective against fixed-wing aircraft and helicopters. They can also be fired while the vehicle is in motion. *United Defense*

grenade launcher on the roof of the vehicle. The RWS is operated by the vehicle commander and fitted with a non-stabilized daylight sight and a thermal night sight. The RWS also carries four M6 smoke grenade launchers. For protection from enemy armored vehicles, the infantry squad of the ICV is armed with Javelin antitank missiles.

The original Army specifications for the ICV called for it to be strong enough to resist 7.62mm ball ammunition and 152mm artillery high-explosive (HE) fragments. The Army also required the ICV contractors to provide an exterior add-on (appliqué) armor kit at a later date that could defeat 7.62mm and 14.5mm armor-piercing (AP) ammunition. GM

An Infantry Combat Vehicle (ICV) version of the Stryker takes part in a training exercise at the Army's NTC. It is armed with an M2HB .50-caliber (12.7mm) machine gun operated by the vehicle commander from within the vehicle's hull. Located directly below the machine gun are smoke grenade launchers with fitted dust covers. *Michael Green*

Defense and GDLS offered an integrated armor solution that provided 14.5mm protection on each vehicle starting with the initial production deliveries of the ICV. There is also an additional add-on armor kit that will eventually be fitted to the ICV that can defeat rocket-propelled grenade launchers (RPGs).

The ICV is just one variant in the Stryker family of vehicles. The Mobile Gun System (MGS) is the second variant, and there are eight additional configurations of

the ICV. They include a reconnaissance vehicle (RV); mortar carrier (MC); commander's vehicle (CV); fire support vehicle (FSV); engineer squad vehicle (ESV); medical evacuation vehicle (MEV); antitank guided missile vehicle (ATGM); and the nuclear, biological, chemical, reconnaissance vehicle (NBCRV).

All the various versions of the Stryker are armed with the same RWS as the ICV. The only exceptions are the ATGM version of the Stryker, which has a

7.62mm M240 machine gun mounted on the vehicle commander's cupola, and the unarmed ambulance version of the Stryker.

The MGS variant carries a 105mm main gun. The MC is fitted with a 120mm mortar. The ATGM carries a TOW II antitank missiles system. As with previous mobile weapon platforms, the Army continues to experiment and mount other types of mission equipment on its fleet of newly acquired wheeled vehicles. Like many of the Army's updated Legacy Force vehicles, the entire Stryker family of vehicles will feature the FBCB2 digital command and control system.

The Stryker is being built in Canada and the United States, and is a variation of the LAV-III armored personnel carrier (APC) used by the Canadian Army. The LAV-III is based on the Piranha III, a wheeled armored vehicle designed by the Swiss firm of Motorwagenfabrik AG (MOWAG). It has enjoyed great worldwide sales success. In 1999, GM Defense acquired MOWAG. The adoption and modification of a foreign-designed military vehicle instead of an American-designed product reflected the Army's desire to avoid the many years of development entailed in the design of a new armored fighting vehicle from scratch. When the American military acquires proven foreign-designed products, it's called "buying-off-the-shelf."

A partnership or joint venture of General Motors Defense and General Dynamics Land Systems (GDLS) originally manufactured the Stryker

The Stryker ICV is almost 23 feet in length, about 9 feet wide, and 8 feet, 8 inches tall. It has full-time four-wheel drive with selective eight-wheel drive if needed. This particular Stryker ICV at the Army's NTC is armed with a Mk. 19 40mm grenade launcher. *Michael Green*

The Stryker Commander's Vehicle (CV) is almost identical in appearance to a Stryker ICV. The only external features that distinguish it from the standard Stryker ICV are the additional radio antennas and the lack of numerous duffel bags that normally dot the exterior of the personnel carrier variant when in the field for extended periods of time. *Michael Green*

family of vehicles. In late 2002, General Dynamics announced that an agreement had been reached to acquire General Motors Defense in a cash deal worth $1.1 billion. With this acquisition, completed in early 2003, General Dynamics became the world's largest supplier of armored combat vehicles. It is anticipated that GDLS will complete the Stryker production order by 2008.

A total of 2,131 vehicles will be used to deploy six Stryker brigade combat teams (SBCTs), spares, and training base requirements at an estimated cost of $4 billion. Each brigade will consist of 3,500 to 4,000 soldiers and will have 309 Stryker vehicles.

The first SBCT achieved initial operational capability in May 2003 and was certified for overseas deployment at the same time. Ultimately, the Army

will field, at the rate of one per year, two SBCTs in Washington State; one each in Alaska, Hawaii, and Louisiana; and one National Guard brigade in Pennsylvania. The Louisiana unit will be configured as a cavalry regiment. The SBCTs are the Medium Combat Force, and the Legacy Force is the Heavy Combat Force. The Army's Light Combat Forces are the light infantry divisions, such as the 10th Mountain Division and specialized units such as the 82nd and 101st Airborne Divisions.

The Army's overall plans call for a 30-year transformation effort that will provide its ground force elements the ability to deploy a combat brigade anywhere in the world within 96 hours, one division in 120 hours, and five divisions within 30 days. The first step in this ongoing process is to form and equip the first six SBCTs by 2008.

An early production LVTP7. LVT stands for Landing Vehicle Tracked. It is readily identified by its rounded front headlight wells. The "P" stands for personnel. The driver sits at the front of the hull on the left side. The vehicle's diesel engine is located at the front of the vehicle's hull to the right of the driver's position. *United Defense*

The Marine Corps had its inventory of LVTP7s rebuilt and upgraded in the early 1980s. Some new vehicles were made (designated LVTP7A1) to reflect the changes to the vehicle's design. The A1 version can be identified by its square headlight wells, as seen in this photograph. *Huck Hagenbuch*

Although the SBCT is optimized for small, limited conflicts, it is designed to engage in the full spectrum of military operations, including major wars, when augmented by other units or as part of a much larger force. The SBCT's capabilities differ significantly from those found in traditional divisional Army brigades. The SBCT relies on advanced command, control, computer, communications, intelligence, surveillance, and reconnaissance (C4ISR) systems purchased from commercial or government sources that enable the brigade personnel to see the entire battlefield and react before they engage the enemy. Its all-weather intelligence and surveillance capabilities, together with its digitized systems, such as the FBCB2, will allow the SBCT to maintain a 24-hour operational tempo.

The SBCTs will be used to develop, test, and validate new doctrine and organizational structures for the Army's ongoing transformation efforts. They will also help implement new combat and leadership development concepts for the Objective Force, the final step in Army transformation.

The Marine Corps renamed its fleet of LVTP7A1s the Assault Amphibious Vehicle Personnel-7A1 (AAVP7A1) in 1976. This is an AAVP7A1 with the new vehicle commander's turret armed with both an M2HB .50-caliber (12.7mm) machine gun and Mk.19 40mm Grenade Launcher. *Hans Halberstadt*

Marine Corps Amphibious Assault Vehicle Personnel (AAVP7A1)

From the mid-1950s until the early 1960s, the Marine Corps depended on a 35-ton amphibious tracked vehicle to ferry Marines between ship and shore. The Landing Vehicle Tracked Personnel-5 (LVTP5) was constructed from thin steel armor. It had a crew of 3 and could carry 25 infantrymen. A large 810-horsepower gasoline engine provided power. The LVTP5 was never very reliable and had limited mobility. In 1964, the Marine Corps decided to replace its amphibious tracked fleet.

FMC proposed an innovative and affordable welded aluminum amphibious personnel carrier powered by a reliable General Motors 400-horsepower diesel truck engine. The new vehicle was lighter than the LVTP5 by 15 tons, and it was more maneuverable in the water and faster on land. In 1969, the Marine Corps awarded FMC a contract to design and build 942 LVTP7 vehicles. The first production LVTP7 was delivered to the Marine Corps in the fall of 1971. The vehicle can carry 21 Marines and is operated by a crew of 3.

As with other armored vehicles, the LVTP7 chassis was the basis for a family of vehicles. Of the four variants

An AAVP7A1 equipped with the P900 appliqué armor kit (AAK) comes out of the surf. The Marine Corps purchased only 189 examples of this armored kit. Field testing of the AAK led to the decision to acquire a more advanced form of add-on armor kit called the enhanced armor appliqué kit (EAAK). *Greg Stewart*

originally planned, only two were ever built: the LVTC7 command vehicle and the LVTR7 recovery vehicle.

On land, the engine propelled the LVT7's tracks through a transmission specifically built for the vehicle by FMC. In the water, the engine powers twin water-jet pumps on either side of the hull near the rear of the vehicle. These pumps push water through special nozzles at a rate of 14,000 gallons per minute. The result is a top forward water speed of about 8 miles per hour. Movement of the vehicle's two tracks also provides some forward momentum in the water.

In the early 1980s, FMC won the contract to upgrade the LVT7 fleet and build 333 additional new vehicles. The upgraded and new vehicles, called LVT7A1s, included a version of the Cummins multi-fuel turbocharged diesel engine used in the Bradley.

The suspension system was also upgraded for better cross-country speed.

In late 1984, the Marine Corps changed the designation to Assault Amphibious Vehicle-7A1 (AAV7A1). The name change was an acknowledgment of the Marines' increasing land combat role. The armament of the LVTP7 and its successors through the AAVP7A1 was a single .50-caliber M2HB machine gun mounted in a small armored turret operated by the vehicle commander. For the AAVP7A1, the Marine Corps awarded a contract to Cadillac Gage to supply 340 turrets to mount a 40mm automatic grenade launcher in addition to the .50-caliber M2HB machine gun. The Marines ordered another 813 identical turrets from AV Technology to retrofit the remaining AAVP7A1s in the inventory.

A Marine Corps AAVP7A1 fitted with the enhanced armor appliqué kit (EAAK) in Somalia in 1993. A bow-plane kit in its stored position is on the lower front of the vehicle. It was installed on the AAVP7A1 fleet to improve the performance when it operated in water with the EAAK. *DVIC*

The basic hull of the AAV7A1 family of vehicles will stand up against only certain types of small-arms fire and artillery fragments. To provide the vehicle with an improved degree of protection, the Marine Corps began to explore the concept of adding extra armor to the exterior of its AAV7A1s in the early 1980s. It took until 1987 before the Marine Corps awarded a contract for 189 kits of add-on armor called the P900 appliqué armor kit (AAK). It consisted of two layers of flat perforated steel armor plates attached to the sides of the AAV7A1 hull. It was capable of defeating 14.5mm machine gun fire. While the AAK kits were built in the United States, the actual designer of the product was an Israeli firm.

The Marine Corps was impressed with the potential of the AAK and ordered 1,317 examples of an improved version, the enhanced appliqué armor kit (EAAK), in 1989. The last EAAK was delivered to

The latest version of the Marine Corps' AAVP7A1 fleet is shown at high speed. It was upgraded under the Reliability and Maintainability/ Rebuild to Standards (RAM/RS) program. The only distinguishing external feature is the relocation of the engine exhaust and muffler from just behind the engine compartment to directly behind the vehicle commander's cupola as seen in this photo. *United Defense*

the Marine Corps in 1993. It consisted of two layers of steel alloy armor with a variety of non-metallic materials sandwiched between them. Unlike the earlier AAK that consisted only of flat armor plates, the EAAK was designed to fit the contours of the vehicle's hull. The EAAK also provides protection to the hull roof of the AAV7A1 and the crew roof hatches. Spall liners on the interior of the vehicle's hull are also part of the EAAK package. Besides protection against 14.5mm machine gun fire, the vehicle and

occupants now have protection from 152mm artillery fragments.

In 2000, the Marine Corps ordered a complete overhaul of the majority of its AAV7A1 fleet. A key upgrade feature is the major components designed for another American military ground vehicle. The AAV family now uses the Bradley's engine, track, and other suspension components. The program is called the Reliability and Maintainability/Rebuild to Standards (RAM/RS), and will be completed in 2003.

CHAPTER 3

WHEELED ARMORED FIREPOWER

Armored Humvees

On March 22, 1983, the U.S. Army Tank Automotive and Armament Command (TACOM) awarded the AM General Division of LTV Aerospace and Defense, now the AM General Corporation, a $1.2 billion contract to build 55,000 High Mobility Multipurpose Wheeled Vehicles (HMMWVs) over a five-year period. TACOM also retained options on another 15,000 vehicles to bring the total number of HMMWVs to 70,000 vehicles. Follow-on contract awards have raised the total number of HMMWVs built by AM General for the American armed forces to almost 142,000 vehicles. The bulk of the HMMWV's fleet is in the Army and the Marine Corps, with much smaller numbers in the Air Force and Navy.

Since HMMWV is a mouthful to pronounce, the vehicle was nicknamed Humvee by the troops, which is now a registered trademark of the AM General Corporation. The vehicle was also called the Hummer, which is now a registered trademark of the General Motors Corporation and has been applied to a new civilian sport-utility vehicle (SUV).

The most numerous Humvee variants in service with the American military today are a variety of non-armored cargo-troop-carrier models. There is also a line of armament carriers configured to mount on a variety of weapon systems that range from machine guns to antitank missiles. All the armament carriers in American military service have polycarbonate

Marine Corps Humvee armament carriers have an extra add-on armor kit affixed to the exterior of their vehicles, including the doors. This covers up the X-shaped pattern seen on the doors of Army or Air Force armament carriers, as is clearly visible in this photograph of a Marine armament carrier. *Michael Green*

A U.S. Army M1026 armament carrier version of the Humvee makes a sharp turn. This particular vehicle is fitted with a front-mounted winch. A member of the crew mans an M249 5.56mm squad automatic weapon (SAW). *AM General*

bullet-resistant windows, also known as transparent armor. The aluminum and fiberglass doors on the armament-carrier versions of the Humvee bear a distinctive X-shaped stamping to increase door rigidity. There is also a composite fiber liner, called E-glass, imbedded in the doors of the armament carriers to resist small-caliber bullet fragments no heavier than 12 grams.

The Marine Corps armament carriers have been equipped with a supplemental armor kit that consists of thin, flat steel armor plates attached to the doors and other surfaces. The steel roof and polycarbonate bullet-resistant windows of the Marine Corps armament carrier version are thicker than those found on Army or Air Force armament carriers. All of these various features provide an additional degree of protection from bullet and artillery fragments up to 44 grams.

As AM General continued to improve the Humvee, it eventually began to build a version designated the M1097 Heavy Humvee in September 1992. In contrast to the earlier versions of the cargo-troop carrier models that had a curb weight of only 5,200

An M1025 armament carrier version of the Humvee in U.S. Army military police service. The hardtop enclosure that covers the entire vehicle from the front windshield to the tailgate is clearly visible in this photograph. Another spotting feature of most Army and Air Force armament carriers is the solid metal doors with an X-shaped pattern stamped into them. *DVIC*

pounds, the Heavy Humvee had a curb weight that was almost double that. To take advantage of this extra weight-carrying capacity, AM General developed a prototype armament carrier version of the Heavy Humvee that featured an enhanced degree of steel armor protection that could withstand 7.62mm ball ammunition at a range of 15 feet or more. It could also hold up against 4-pound antitank/antipersonnel mines. The vehicle's windows were made of non-spalling ballistic glass. A small number of armored Heavy Humvees produced by AM General were quickly sold to an unnamed foreign buyer, but the American military did not purchase any armored Heavy Humvees.

In April 1993, the Army deployed troops and equipment to the Eastern African country of Somalia in support of United Nations peacekeeping duties. The Army quickly realized the crews of its armament-carrier Humvees were vulnerable because almost every male citizen carried a small-arms weapon. To provide its soldiers with a better-protected Humvee, the Army solicited AM General to expedite production of its armored armament carrier on the Heavy Humvee chassis.

To meet the Army's needs, AM General teamed with the O'Gara-Hess & Eisenhardt Armoring Company (OHE), a long-time builder of armored vehicles for the civilian market. AM General supplied the Heavy

The U.S. Army M1114 seen in this photo is armed with a shield-protected Mk. 19 40mm automatic grenade launcher. Many of the M1114s in the Army's inventory can be found in Military Police (MP) units. Besides traffic control the Army's MP are responsible for rear area security and prisoners of war (POWs). *O'Gara-Hess & Eisenhardt*

Hummer chassis, and OHE armored the vehicles to Army specifications. OHE had its first prototype vehicle, the XM1109, ready for Army approval in June 1993. The Army liked the prototype and awarded OHE a contract in August 1993 to build several test vehicles. These test vehicles underwent a series of ballistic tests in December 1993 that subjected them to a variety of small arms fire and mine blasts. The Army was extremely pleased with the test results and awarded OHE a production contract. The first of 159 production vehicles was delivered to the Army in January 1994.

The first XM1109s were deployed to Somalia in May 1994 to the delight of the troops who received them. They were also deployed to the small Caribbean country of Haiti to assist Army troops stationed there for peacekeeping duties. A ring mount on the roof of the vehicle could be fitted with a 7.62mm M60 machine gun, a .50-caliber M2HB machine gun, or a Mk. 19 40mm automatic grenade launcher. While AM General and OHE both offered the Army a roof-mounted, open-topped, armored cupola for the vehicle's gunner on the XM1109, it was

The distinguishing features of the M1114 include the air-conditioning vents on the right side of the rear trunk cover and the extended headlight housing that sticks out from the front of the vehicle's radiator. These features are not present on the standard Humvee armament carriers. *O'Gara-Hess & Eisenhardt*

not an option selected by the Army for its production of the XM1109.

The Army recognized some limitations of the XM1109 and requested OHE and AM General to develop a more robust vehicle. Their work resulted in the design of the XM1114, a prototype up-armored Humvee armament carrier based on the turbocharged XM1113 chassis. OHE based the design on the new AM General version of the Humvee called the Enhanced Capacity Vehicle (ECV) that started to roll off AM General's assembly line in 1994. The vehicle had a curb weight of 12,100 pounds. To push the extra weight around, the ECV had a more powerful diesel engine than earlier versions of the Humvee. It also had a strengthened drivetrain and suspension system to allow for additional payload.

The XM1114's upgraded ballistic armor offered protection from 7.62mm armor-piercing ammunition at 100-meter standoff range, and from a contact-detonated 12-pound mine blast under the front tire of the vehicle. The rear portion of the crew compartment could stand against a 4-pound contact-detonated mine blast. The armor protection of the vehicle also protected its crew from 155mm artillery air-burst fragments at a range of over 100 meters.

In September 1995, the M1114 prototype vehicle successfully passed a series of ballistic and mine-blast tests conducted by the Army at Aberdeen Proving Ground, Maryland. A production contract soon followed, and OHE shipped the first M1114s to the Army in January 1996. By October 1996, OHE had delivered over 500 M1114s. The Army currently has a fleet of over 2,900 M1114s in worldwide service. The vehicle can be armed with a 5.56mm M240 machine gun, a .50-caliber M2HB machine gun, or a Mk. 19 40mm grenade launcher.

The Air Force approached the O'Gara Company in 1996 to provide its base security police units with

In order to pass all the Army's requirements, the M1114 was subjected to a wide array of tests simulating real-world threats it might encounter in service. This dramatic photo shows an M1114 at the moment a contact mine of unknown size exploded under the front wheels of the vehicle. *O'Gara-Hess & Eisenhardt*

an armored Humvee similar to the Army's M1114, but specially designed and tailored to its own specific needs. The result was the M1116, which entered Air Force service in 1998. Unlike the Army's M1114, the Air Force's M1116 has a roof-mounted, open-top armored gun platform that provides the vehicle's gunner with 360-degree protection from a variety of weapons. Until recently, the only armor protection for the vehicle's gunner was the folded two-piece hatch stored behind the weapon ring mount. There is now a small, flat, armored shield that can be mounted in front of the gunner's position on the Army's M1114.

A key external difference between the Army's M1114 and the Air Force's M1116 is the configuration of the vehicle's rear cargo bay. The Army's M1114 features the same hatchback roof design as seen on all other armament carriers. In contrast, the Air Force asked for extra storage room in the rear cargo bay of the M1116 and had OHE design a box-like enclosure to cover the rear cargo bay of its vehicle. The Air Force currently has about 500 of the M1116 vehicles in service. Like the M1114, it can be armed with machine guns or a Mk. 19 40mm automatic grenade launcher. An M-82A1 Barret .50-caliber sniper rifle can also be

The M1116 seen in this photograph is employed by U.S. Air Force Security detachments to protect American military air bases around the world. It is powered by a 6.5-liter turbocharged 190-horsepower diesel engine. It rides on a suspension system that consists of an independent double A-frame with open-end coil springs and hydraulic shock absorbers. *O'Gara-Hess & Eisenhardt*

mounted on the armored gun platform of the M1116. Since their introduction, the armored Humvees, M1114 and M1116, have become the vehicles of choice for many Department of Energy (DOE) locations and several foreign countries.

M117 Armored Security Vehicle (ASV)

In December 1995, Cadillac Gage, now a division of the Textron Marine & Land Systems Corporation, was awarded a contract by the Army to build four prototypes of a new four-wheeled armored security vehicle (ASV) for the Military Police (MP) units. The company

delivered the four prototype XM1117 vehicles to the Army in February 1997. The Army vehicle tests were completed by October 1997. This led to a five-year production contract for 94 vehicles in March 1999. The vehicle was standardized as the M1117 and given the official name "Guardian."

The 15-ton Guardian is a four-wheel-drive vehicle with an all-wheel independent suspension system. Its six-speed automatic transmission is connected to a 260-horsepower Cummins diesel engine that gives it a top speed of about 63 miles per hour on paved roads. It has a cruising range of about 400 miles. The four

large tires on the vehicles have run-flat inserts that will allow them to operate at least an extra 25 miles if punctured. The crew consists of the vehicle commander, gunner, and driver. There are 26 Guardians in an MP Company. Current plans call for the eventual development of eight companies of ASVs (208 vehicles) for the Army's MP Branch.

U.S. Marine Corps Light Armored Vehicle (LAV) Family

A series of dramatic events occurred in 1979 that rattled the entire world order. They included the overthrow of the pro-American leader of Iran by an Islamic radical movement, and the seizure by Iranian students of the American Embassy and its staff. This was quickly followed by a Soviet invasion of Afghanistan in December. Because the bulk of America's ground military power was designed to stop a possible Soviet invasion of Western Europe, it consisted primarily of well-armed heavy armor vehicles that were ill suited to respond quickly to other areas of conflict around the globe. To address this shortcoming, America's military leaders created a new joint-service military organization called the Rapid Deployment Force (RDF) in 1980. The RDF was later renamed the Central Command.

Several requirements were set for the new RDF. The ground-forces elements had to have vehicles light enough to be carried within existing transport aircraft, or carried as a sling load by transport helicopters then in service. While the U.S. Marine Corps' inventory of tanks and amphibious assault vehicles at the time was more than adequate to seize a hostile shore, they were not light or small enough to fit within the RDF guidelines. To rectify this shortcoming, the U.S. Marine Corps (USMC) looked for an off-the-shelf light armored vehicle (LAV) that could be configured to serve many different battlefield roles.

The hull of the Guardian and its weapon-armed turret is made of steel-alloy armor that will protect it from many types of small-arms fire and artillery fragments. The vehicle's turret is armed with an M2HB .50-caliber machine gun and an Mk. 19 40mm automatic grenade launcher. *U.S. Army*

As its designation indicates, the Marine Corps LAV-25 is armed with the turret-mounted M242 25mm automatic cannon. It is stabilized in elevation and traverse, which allows it to be fired accurately while on the move. One of the vehicle's four scouts is standing up in the rear hull of the LAV-25 pictured on a road at Camp Pendleton, California. *Hans Halberstadt*

After evaluating many possible contenders for the USMC's LAV, an initial production contract was issued to General Motors of Canada in September 1982. The product they had submitted for Marine Corps approval was a license-built copy of the Piranha I, an eight-wheeled armored vehicle designed and developed by the Swiss firm of Motorwagenfabrik AG (MOWAG). The development of the Piranha I series dated from the 1970s, and the first prototype vehicles appeared in 1972. The vehicles built for the Marine Corps LAV program are slightly different from the original Swiss-designed Piranha I.

The eight-wheeled Piranha I weighed 14 tons and was powered by a General Motors diesel engine that produced 275 horsepower. On land, the vehicle had a top road speed of 60 miles per hour and a maximum operational range of 475 miles. The Piranha also could cross calm inland waterways by two propellers at the rear of the vehicle. The top water speed of the vehicle was 6 miles per hour. The steel armor hull (and turret when fitted) of the Piranha I protected against 7.62mm ball ammunition.

In Marine Corps service, the LAV comes in eight different configurations. Four of them were designed as weapon platforms (nicknamed shooters), while the other four were configured to provide support functions. The support function variants of the LAV include the LAV-L (logistics), LAV-R (recovery), LAV-C2 (command), and the LAV-EW (electronic warfare).

The weapon-carrying versions of the Marine Corps LAV program included the LAV-25 (25mm gun-armed turret), LAV-AT (antitank), LAV-AD (air defense), and LAV-M (mortar, covered in chapter four). The Marine Corps extensively tested a fifth weapon-armed version of the LAV equipped with a 105mm main gun. However, Congress never provided

The LAV-25 is 21 feet long and 7 feet, 2-1/2 inches wide. The height of the vehicle is 8 feet, 2-1/2 inches. It is air transportable by all the Air Force's current transport aircraft. The LAV-25 can also be carried in sling beneath the Marine Corps' CH-53E Super Sea Stallion helicopter, as seen here. *DVIC*

A Marine Corps LAV-25 taking part in training exercises conducted in Norway in the late 1980s. The M242 25mm automatic cannon mounted in the LAV-25 can fire either an armor piercing discarding sabot (APDS) or high explosive incendiary tracer (HEI-T) round at a rate of up to 200 rounds per minute. *DVIC*

A Marine Corps LAV-AT with its TOW under armor (TUA) turret, nicknamed the Hammerhead, in its firing position. In addition to the two missile launching tubes that are located in the Hammerhead, there are gunner's optics. These include a day sight as well as a thermal night sight. *Greg Stewart*

funding for its procurement despite requests from the Marine Corps.

The LAV-25 had a two-person, power-operated turret armed with an M242 25mm automatic cannon called the Chain Gun, and two 7.62mm M240 machine guns. While there is room in the rear hull compartment of the LAV-25 for up to six infantrymen, the Marines eventually decided to use the vehicle as a reconnaissance asset instead of an armored personnel carrier. As a reconnaissance vehicle, the LAV-25 normally carries four Marine scouts in the rear hull compartment. The crew of the LAV-25 consists of the driver in the front hull, and the vehicle commander and gunner in the turret. The Marine Corps was supplied with 422 LAV-25s between 1983 and 1987.

The LAV-AT has a power-operated turret that contains two TOW II missile launchers and their associated sighting equipment, including a thermal imaging sight. The upper portion of the sight, housed in the armored launcher assembly, can be rotated 360 degrees and raised or lowered by a hydraulic trunnion assembly. The launcher's unofficial nickname is the Hammerhead. When the vehicle is in transit, the Hammerhead is

Shown in its stored position on a Marine Corps LAV-AT is the TOW under armor (TUA) turret. The crew of the LAV-AT always seek out a firing position that exposes only the upper portion of the launcher to enemy observation. *GM Defense*

The Marine Corps depends on its inventory of LAV-AD to protect its ground forces from aerial attack. This photo shows an LAV-AD in its firing position, with its 25mm GAU12 five-barrel, Gatling-type gun and its quadruple Stinger missile launcher ready to engage a low-flying aerial target. *GD Armament Division*

stored on the rear deck of the vehicle's hull facing rearward. When the vehicle's gunner, located in the hull of the vehicle, is ready to fire the TOW missiles, the Hammerhead is raised and the TOW missiles are pointed at the target. In its raised position, the Hammerhead extends 5 feet above the vehicle's hull. This allows the LAV-AT crew to keep the vehicle's hull under cover when engaging targets.

When the gunner on the LAV-AT has fired off the two ready-round missiles in the Hammerhead, it is tilted rearward and reloaded through an overhead hatch on the roof of the vehicle's rear hull compartment. The LAV-AT can carry 14 extra TOW missiles in the rear hull compartment. Besides the gunner, the LAV-AT is crewed by a driver, vehicle commander, and a loader. There is normally a 7.62mm M240 machine

73

A prototype of the Stryker (MGS) armed with a 105mm main gun is pictured at an Army test range. The production version of the vehicle planned for introduction in Army service by 2005 will differ slightly in its external appearance from the prototype version pictured. *U.S. Army*

gun mounted on the vehicle commander's cupola located in front of the Hammerhead. The Marine Corps acquired 96 LAV-ATs.

The LAV-AD entered Marine Corps service in 1997. Its crew consists of a vehicle commander, gunner, and driver. While the original Marine Corps requirement called for production of a total of 125 LAV-ADs, Congress funded the production of only 17 vehicles, and the last was delivered in 1998. The LAV-AD is equipped with a General Electric (GE)-designed and -built two-person, power-operated turret. It is armed with a GAU-12/U 25mm Gatling Gun and eight Stinger surface-to-air missiles divided between two separate missile launching pods. The LAV-AD carries an additional eight Stinger missiles in its rear hull compartment as reloads. Lockheed Martin Ordinance Systems (now General Dynamics Armament System

Division) was awarded the contract to assemble the LAV-ADs for the Marine Corps.

The Marine Corps obtained funding to upgrade its entire family of LAV vehicles with a service life extension program (SLEP) in 2002. It will extend the useful life of the LAV family of vehicles until 2015. The actual upgrading process will occur between 2003 and 2004. These upgrades will include several important survivability enhancements and electrical system upgrades to the entire USMC LAV family of vehicles. The SLEP will replace the passive night sight on the LAV-25 with a more capable thermal imaging sight.

Stryker Weapon Platforms

The Mobile Gun System (MGS) and the Antitank Guided Missile (ATGM) vehicles are part of the Stryker family of vehicles. The first production examples of the Stryker ATGM were delivered to the Army in 2002. The MGS is currently in development and is expected to enter into Army service by 2005.

The principal function of the Stryker MGS will be to provide Stryker company commanders with the ability to support their assaulting infantry elements with rapid and lethal direct fire upon enemy defensive positions. The MGS consists of a GDLS-designed turret mounted on top of a Stryker chassis. The turret is armed with an M68A1 105mm rifled main gun and a coaxial 7.62mm M240 machine gun. The M68E1 main gun is the same weapon that was mounted on the M60 series of main battle tanks and the first two versions of the M1 Abrams tank. Because the turret on the Stryker MGS is fully stabilized, the weapons can be accurately fired at targets while the vehicle is in motion. The 105mm main gun can fire a variety of ammunition types including armor-piercing, high-explosive antitank, antipersonnel, and a high-explosive plastic round to destroy enemy bunkers.

To keep the height of the Stryker MGS turret to a minimum so it can fit within the confines of American military transport planes such as the C-130 Hercules, the turret has a special low-profile design that projects only 3 feet above the roof of the Stryker chassis. The two-person turret crew consists of the vehicle commander and gunner, who operates the main gun and the coaxial machine gun from within the turret basket located within the Stryker's hull. The human loader has been replaced with an autoloader that has access to 18 main gun rounds stored within the vehicle's hull. The MGS also has an M2HB .50-caliber machine gun that is independently mounted at the vehicle commander's position.

The Stryker ATGM vehicle is armed with the TOW II antitank missile system. Unlike the missile launcher assembly on the LAV-AT (nicknamed the Hammerhead) that is raised into its firing position by a hydraulic trunnion assembly, the missile launcher assembly of the Stryker ATGM, called the Elevated TOW System (ETS), is raised vertically by a mechanical screw-driven mast. Once it is in its firing position, the ETS can be rotated 360 degrees. The ETS is lowered for transport or motor pool storage purposes only.

A Stryker ATGM in a defensive overwatch position during a training exercise conducted at the Army's NTC in March 2003. On a live-fire range or in combat, the radio antennas located on the top of the vehicle's hull are folded down and locked into position. The vehicle commander's M240 7.62mm machine also folds sideways before a TOW is fired. *Michael Green*

INDIRECT ARMORED FIRE SUPPORT

A key element of the Army's Legacy Force is its ability to deliver massive and accurate indirect fire. The indirect fire armored fighting vehicles deliver their ammunition by way of cannons, rockets, missiles, and mortars.

Of the four methods of delivery at the disposal of the Legacy Force, the cannons (tube artillery) are most often used to deliver the greatest number of rounds to small, high-value targets. Tube artillery is known for its combination of range and accuracy. Modern rockets have a slight edge in range, but lack a cannon's accuracy. Rockets are generally reserved for counter-battery fire on enemy artillery units where accuracy is not critical.

Guided missiles are extremely accurate and have more than double the range of tube and rocket artillery. However, they are much more expensive and are reserved for only the most important battlefield targets. Mortars are used for short-range targets.

M109A6 Paladin

Since the 1960s, the M109 series has been the mainstay of the Army's self-propelled artillery fleet. The aluminum alloy armored hull provides protection from artillery fragments and small-arms fire. All M109 versions have a turret armed with a 155mm howitzer. Over the decades, the M109 series has been progressively improved to maintain its place as the predominant indirect-fire weapon on the modern battlefield.

In 1979, the Army wanted to develop a new series of advanced self-propelled howitzers to replace the M109 series. As cost estimates for a new fleet escalated, the Army decided to upgrade the M109 series once

An Army National Guard M109A2 on a firing range at Camp Roberts, California, in 1988. Production of the original M109 self-propelled 155mm howitzer began in 1962. The A1 version appeared in 1970, and the A2 version arrived in 1976. The 109A2 had onboard storage for 36 rounds of ammunition. *Michael Green*

CHAPTER 4

An impressive fireball created by the firing of a high-explosive round from an M109A3's 155mm howitzer is seen in this nighttime photograph. With a well-trained crew, a maximum rate of fire of four rounds could be kept up for three minutes. The sustained rate of fire of the crew of an M109A3 is only one round per minute. *Greg Stewart*

again. The upgrades from the M109A4 to the A5 version included a more powerful 155mm howitzer. The upgrade program started in 1992 with the entire Army National Guard M109 Howitzer fleet being upgraded to the A5 version.

Simultaneously with the conversion of the Army National Guard's M109A4s to the A5 configuration, the active component of the Army fielded another version of the M109 series called the M109A6 Paladin. It combines the battle-proven M109 series chassis with a larger turret designed and built by United Defense. The 155mm howitzer can reach targets up to 14 miles away with standard artillery ammunition. With rocket-assisted artillery ammunition, targets can be destroyed at ranges up to 18 miles. For comparison, the original M109 from the early 1960s had a maximum range of 9 miles with standard artillery ammunition.

A fully automatic computer fire-control system is unique to the Paladin. It is connected to an integrated inertial navigation system with an embedded Global Positioning System (GPS). These electronic devices allow the vehicle to receive a fire mission via radio and immediately compute all needed firing data while on the move. At the same time, the Paladin's computers put together the firing data and direct the vehicle's driver to an optimal firing position.

Once at the firing position, the vehicle's onboard computer automatically unlocks the 155mm howitzer barrel from its travel lock, points the cannon in the chosen direction, and fires the first round of ammunition.

A U.S. Army M109A6 Paladin based at Fort Hood, Texas, operates at speed. The vehicle weighs 32 tons and is 29 feet, 11 inches long. It has a width of 10 feet, 4 inches and is 10 feet, 9 inches tall. It is powered by a 440-horsepower diesel engine and has a top road speed of 40 miles per hour. *Hans Halberstadt*

This happens in just under 60 seconds after the vehicle stops. After that, the Paladin gunner can fire up to four rounds per minute for about three minutes. Once the firing mission is completed, the howitzer barrel is automatically returned to its travel lock, and the Paladin leaves the site before the enemy can react with counter-battery fire.

The 39 artillery projectiles and 44 propellant charges for the Paladin's howitzer are stored in a full-width steel armored bustle behind the vehicle's turret. Additional artillery projectiles and propellant charges are carried in a separate vehicle, the M992A2 Field Artillery Ammunition Support Vehicle (FAASV). Each Paladin has an FAASV assigned to it. The FAASV is a Paladin without its turret or howitzer. The interior of

the FAASV can store 93 projectiles and 96 propellant charges. Projectiles and propellant charges are moved between vehicles either manually or by a conveyer belt system carried onboard the FAASV. The Army National Guard doesn't have FAASVs and instead uses M548s, an unarmored version of the M113, to carry additional ammunition for its fleet of M109A5s.

The 155mm howitzer on the Paladin can fire a variety of conventional and unconventional artillery rounds. Since conventional munitions have no mechanism to change course after they are fired, they are called dumb rounds. In contrast, smart rounds are munitions that can change trajectory on their way to a target. The dumb rounds fired by the M109A6 Paladin and the National Guard's M109A5 include high explosive (HE) rounds that are deadly to unarmored vehicles or troops in the open. Both vehicles can fire rounds that eject small antitank or antipersonnel mines as they fly over a target area. This family of scatterable mines (FASCAM) is used to slow down an attacking force of armored vehicles or infantry. M109s can also fire smoke rounds to mask the advance or withdrawal of American ground forces.

The M712 Copperhead is the current smart round for the M109A5 and A6. It is guided to its target by a laser designator operated by a soldier who has a direct view of the target. The two biggest drawbacks of the Copperhead are its short three-and-a-half-mile range and its inability to operate in rain or fog. A possible replacement for the Copperhead is the Sense and Destroy Armor (SADARM). It carries two submunitions that are ejected over a target. The submunitions use onboard sensors to identify a target and fire an explosively formed penetrator (EFP), which is very effective at destroying lightly armored vehicles, but less effective against heavily armored tanks.

The Army will soon use the XM982 Excalibur extended range guided projectile, a new, long-range smart artillery round. The Excalibur has a maximum range of 24 miles. It contains a Global Positioning System (GPS) and an inertial measurement unit (IMU)

An impressive formation of M109A6 Paladins line up on a firing range at Fort Hood, Texas. Some of the features found on the vehicle include an automatic fire-control system, a navigation system, and protection from nuclear, biological, and chemical weapons. An onboard computer pinpoints equipment problems for easy maintenance. *Hans Halberstadt*

The vehicle commander's position in an M109A6 Paladin, as well as an 155mm round ready to be loaded into the weapon's breech. The Paladin has storage space for 39 rounds of 155mm ammunition. *Hans Halberstadt*

An M992A2 field artillery ammunition support vehicle (FAASV) is pictured during field training exercises at Fort Hood, Texas. The FAASV is a modified M109 chassis adapted for the role of artillery ammunition re-supply vehicle. In place of the 360-degree rotating turret on the M109A6 Paladin, the FAASV has a fixed superstructure. *Hans Halberstadt*

to make it extremely accurate. Three Excalibur rounds can do the job that once would have taken about 150 dumb artillery rounds to accomplish. The high cost of artillery smart rounds will always limit their use to only the most important targets.

M270 Multiple-Launch Rocket System (MLRS)

The Army introduced a new armored self-propelled multiple-tube rocket launcher in 1977. The primary MLRS mission was counter-battery fire. Secondary missions included suppression of enemy air defense systems and interdiction fires against targets such as troops, unarmored equipment, and command and control centers.

Two companies were awarded MLRS development contracts to build prototypes of the new rocket artillery system. Loral Vought Systems Corporation won the production contract in 1980 as the prime contractor. The first production units were delivered to the Army in 1982. By the time production of the M270 MLRS was completed in 1995, the Army and the Army National Guard had over 800 units in service. The Army also calls the M270 MLRS a self-propelled loader/launcher (SPLL).

The M270 MLRS consists of an M269 launcher loader module (LLM) that sits in the rear cargo bay of an M933 Carrier Vehicle. The large, box-like launcher is raised and lowered with hydraulics. The launcher contains two bays, each of which houses a pod containing six 227mm M26 rockets in its sealed launching tubes. Each rocket is about 13 feet long and weighs 676 pounds. As with all rockets, the M26 is a dumb round. The flight trajectory depends on the elevation of the LLM launcher tube at the time the rockets are fired.

There are 644 small, individual M77 dual-purpose improved conventional munitions (DPICM) inside the warhead section of the M26 rocket. The dual-purpose designation means the munitions are equally effective

The M992A2 FAASV has a crew of five and is comparable to the M109A6 Paladin in speed, mobility, and survivability. Each Paladin is assigned an FAASV. Pictured at the Army's NTC is a Paladin with its supporting FAASV parked directly behind it. *Greg Stewart*

Before an M992A2 FAASV crew reloads an M109A6 Paladin, they open the rear access doors of their vehicle, as seen here. They then erect a fold-out, power-operated conveyor belt device that will link the two vehicles. *Greg Stewart*

With an M992A2 FAASV parked directly behind an M109A6 Paladin, the crewmen of the FAASV place 155mm rounds onto the power-operated conveyor belt, as seen in this photo. The rounds are transported into the Paladin while the crews of both vehicles remain under armor protection. *DVIC*

An Army M270 armored vehicle-mounted rocket launcher (MLRS) is ready to fire. The carrier vehicle is an elongated version of the Bradley Fighting Vehicle (BFV). The vehicle's three-man crew operates the vehicle and fires the rockets from the safety of the aluminum-alloy armor cab seen in the photo. *DVIC*

against armored targets and personnel. The DPICMs can be carried to a maximum range of 20 miles before they leave the M26 rocket. Once the rocket is directly over the target area at roughly 4,000 feet elevation, an electronic time fuse ignites a charge that pops the warhead section open.

The submunitions are encased in Styrofoam blocks. When the warhead section opens, the Styrofoam quickly begins to shred and scatters the submunitions over the target area. Each submunition has a drag ribbon that acts as a drogue parachute to slow its descent and point its warhead section downwards. The submunitions can penetrate up to 4 inches of armor if they strike an armored vehicle. If they don't

hit an object as they descend, they explode into fragments on impact with the ground. Fragments from the steel body of the submunitions have a kill radius of about 50 feet against personnel in the open.

During a full-load launch of 12 rockets, one M270 MLRS can saturate an area with almost 8,000 submunitions. The few Iraqi troops who survived an MLRS/M77 attack during Operation Desert Storm in 1991 called it the "steel rain." The Army has upgraded the M26 rocket with a more powerful motor for targets up to 28 miles away. The new rocket can carry M77 submunitions, 28 AT2 parachute-stabilized antitank mines, or 6 sense and destroy armor (SADARM) submunitions.

An M26 tactical rocket leaves an M270 MLRS launch pod container. The MLRS rocket follows a ballistic, free-flight (unguided) trajectory to its target. Propulsion for the M26 rocket is provided by a solid-propellant rocket motor that, once ignited, provides thrust for about two seconds. *DVIC*

A guided missile was developed for the M270 MLRS that can destroy targets at even longer ranges than the extended-range M26 rocket. In 1986, Loral Vought Systems Corporation was awarded a contract to develop the M39 Army Tactical Missile System (ATACMS) Block I. The M39 has a useful range of 62 miles. Loral delivered the first production units to the Army in 1991.

Each ATACMS missile is 13 feet long, 2 feet in diameter, and weighs 3,687 pounds. The M270 MLRS turret can carry and launch only two ATACMS at a time. Each ATACMS missile is enclosed in a sealed pod with the same outside dimensions as the standard six-rocket pod. The Block I ATACMS carries 950 M74 antipersonnel/antimateriel submunitions. The Block II ATACMS carries only 275 M74 submunitions, but it can achieve a range of 186 miles. A GPS navigation system makes the extreme range of the Block II version possible.

The Block II ATACMS missile can carry 13 brilliant anti-armor technology (BAT) submunitions. Unlike the dumb M74 submunitions, BATs are self-guided submunitions that glide from the missile warhead section to the vicinity of an enemy tank formation. Each BAT then employs an acoustic sensor to select an individual vehicle from the formation and heads directly toward that target. During the last stage of flight, the BAT employs a terminal infrared seeker to identify the target by its heat signature. The BAT then uses a tandem shaped-charge warhead to destroy the target.

The M933 Carrier that acts as the automotive chassis for the M270 MLRS system is 22 feet, 11 inches long; 8 feet, 6 inches tall at the front cab; and 6 feet, 9 inches wide. It shares its powertrain and running gear with the Bradley Fighting Vehicle family. The three-person crew consists of the section leader, gunner, and driver. They operate the vehicle from a front-mounted

Once the crew of an M270 MLRS has fired off its onboard allotment of M26 rockets, the crew can reload the launcher with fresh six-rocket launch-pod containers without outside assistance. This is accomplished with the self-contained boom and hoist assemblies mounted inside the M269 launcher loader module (LLM), as seen in operation in this photo. *DVIC*

cab made of lightweight aluminum alloy armor plate that offers protection from artillery fragments and small-arms fire.

M270 MLRS launch vehicles employ shoot-and-move tactics to enhance survivability. Launcher crews use the onboard electronic fire control system (FCS) to download mission details while positioned in a hide area. Then, they quickly move to a launch area, recalculate based on the new position, fire up to 12 rockets, and leave the launch area, all within three minutes. Although the launcher vehicle has a three-person crew for optimal performance, a single crewmember can perform all these operations if needed.

The M270 MLRS was beginning to show its age by the late 1990s. Most of the electronic hardware was no longer in production, and the software was obsolete. Another problem that became apparent during Operation Desert Storm in 1991 was the slow reload time. This is a problem common to all rocket artillery. Highly mobile enemy formations could easily move to new positions during the time it took to reload the rocket launcher. To address these problems, the Army deployed the first of the new M270A1 MLRS units in 2000.

The biggest improvement in the M270A1 upgrade was the new fire-control system. The new system is

Replacements of the six-rocket launch pods for the M270 MLRS are provided by the M985 HEMTT truck and M989 HEMAT trailer seen here. The M985 truck is equipped with a 5,400-pound lift capacity material-handling crane located at the rear of the vehicle. It can be traversed 360 degrees to unload both the re-supply vehicle and trailer. *DVIC*

compatible with the current range of rockets and missiles and also has the growth potential to handle new rockets and missiles being designed for the M270A1 MLRS. Unlike the older fire-control system built on its own operating system, the new system uses Microsoft Windows as its software platform. A GPS-aided navigation system for the launcher was included to supplement the existing inertial position-navigation system. The combination of improvements allows the M270A1 MLRS crew to aim the launcher in just 16 seconds. The M270 launcher took 93 seconds to aim.

Reload time has been shortened somewhat thanks to a faster launcher drive system.

Self-Propelled Tracked Mortars: M1064A3

The Army fielded its first self-propelled armored mortar vehicle during World War II. It consisted of an 81mm mortar mounted in the rear compartment of either an M2 or M3 half-track. As early as 1945, the Army searched for a suitable full-tracked armored chassis on which to mount a larger 107mm mortar. It took until 1956 before that desire became reality with

The M270 MLRS can launch the Army Tactical Missile System (ATACMS), as seen in this photo. The ATACMS is a conventional ballistic missile that can strike deep targets beyond the range of both existing cannon (tube) artillery or rocket systems. *United Defense*

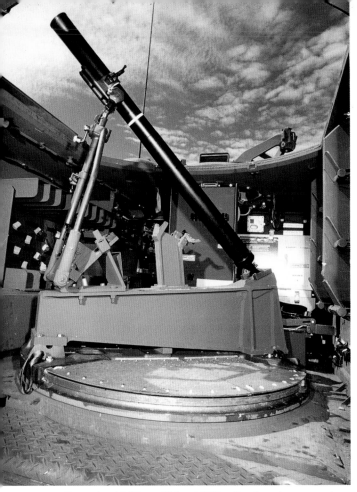

From the 1960s until the 1980s, the Army's armored and mechanized infantry divisions depended on the M125 series mortar carrier. The M29 81mm mortar was mounted on the M125 for short-range indirect fire support. The mortar's rotating turntable and the elevated platform it was mounted on is visible in this photo. *United Defense*

the full-tracked M84 mortar carrier, armed with a 107mm mortar in its rear hull compartment. The M84 was a variant of the M59 APC series of vehicles.

In 1961 the M84 was replaced by two mortar-carrier variants based on the M113 APC family of vehicles. The two self-propelled mortars were the M125, armed with an 81mm mortar, and the M106, armed with a 107mm mortar. Both mortar carriers had a six-person crew. The mortars were mounted in the rear hull compartments. Like the rest of the Army's inventory of M113-series vehicles, they were progressively upgraded to the A1 and, later, to the A2 versions.

The Army pulled its fleet of about 500 M125A2 81mm mortar carriers from service during the 1980s. The surplus chassis were converted to other uses. The M106A2 fleet of roughly 1,000 vehicles was retained and the chassis was upgraded to M113A3 standards. A new Israeli-designed 120mm mortar was included in this upgrade process to replace the Army's aging 107mm mortar. The 120mm mortar is designated the M121 Battalion Mortar System (BMS). The combination chassis and mortar upgrades resulted in a new designation—the M1064A3 mortar carrier. Conversion of the Army's fleet of M106A2s into the M1064A3 was accomplished between 1988 and 1996.

The M1064A3 has a crew of five: squad leader, gunner, assistant gunner, ammo bearer, and driver. The vehicle carries 69 rounds of 120mm ammunition. A well-trained crew can fire up to 16 rounds during the first minute, and four rounds per minute after that. The 120mm mortar has a top effective range of about 24,000 feet. When the M1064A3 vehicle moves from one location to another, the mortar is lowered into a horizontal position and the roof hatches are closed to make it almost impossible to distinguish it from many other types of M113A3s. The mortar can be dismounted from the vehicle and fired from the ground, if necessary.

Ammunition for the Army's 120mm mortar includes the M934A1 high explosive (HE) smoke round and a new infrared illumination round that provides enhanced night fighting capability. New smart-munition developments for the 120mm mortar include a rocket-propelled extended-range munition, a precision-guided mortar munition (PGMM), and the dual-purpose improved conventional munition (DPICM).

A new mortar fire-control system (MFCS) for the M1064A3 will provide Paladin-like fire-control capability to the vehicle and allow it to link digitally with other Army ground and aerial platforms. With the MFCS, the M1064A3 crew will be able to begin a firing mission in less than 60 seconds, instead of the current 8 to 12 minutes standard.

An Army M1064A3 mortar carrier, with its rear hull ramp in the down position, allows an unobstructed view into the interior of the vehicle. The very large 120mm mortar is mounted on a rotating turntable. There is storage space in the vehicle for 69 mortar bombs. *United Defense*

The tip of the M252 81mm mortar mounted within the center of the vehicle is barely visible in this photo of a Marine Corps LAV-M. Like the 81mm mortar that was mounted in the Army's M125 Mortar Carrier vehicle, it is mounted on a rotating turntable. *Hans Halberstadt*

Self-Propelled Wheeled Mortar Carriers: Stryker Mortar Carrier (MC) and LAV-M

The Marine Corps fielded the light armored vehicle (LAV) family of wheeled vehicles back in the early 1980s. Among the numerous variants was a mortar carrier vehicle designated the LAV-M. The LAV-M carries an 81mm mortar in the center of the vehicle. There is space within the LAV-M for 90 rounds of 81mm ammunition. The usual mix is 68 HE rounds, 9 smoke rounds, and 13 illuminating rounds. The crew of five includes a driver, vehicle commander, and a three-person mortar squad. The LAV-M also carries an M240 7.62mm machine gun on the commander's cupola for vehicle self-protection.

The M121 Battalion Mortar System (BMS) is one of the weapons mounted on the Army's new Stryker family of 19-ton wheeled armored vehicles. In the Model A, the original version of the Stryker mortar carrier (MC) released in 2002, the 120mm mortar cannot be fired from within the confines of

A picture taken at the U.S. Army's National Training Center in March 2003 shows the Stryker mortar carrier Model A with its 120mm mortar deployed in its firing position with a two-man crew behind the vehicle. When the vehicle is in transit between firing positions, the mortar barrel is stored within the hull. The base plate for the mortar is stored on the exterior of the vehicle's hull. *Michael Green*

the vehicle. Instead, it has to be dismounted from the vehicle by its crew and erected before firing. This process is far more time-consuming than being able to fire the mortar from within the vehicle, and it leaves the mortar, crew, and vehicle highly exposed to counter-battery fire.

The builders of the Stryker family of vehicles, General Dynamic Land System (GDLS) division in partnership with GM Defense, was well aware of the battlefield shortcomings of the Model A Stryker mortar carrier vehicle. They had already begun to develop an improved version of the vehicle, the Model B, that would allow the 120mm mortar to be fired from within the vehicle by its crew through an overhead hatch in the roof of the hull. The crew of the Model B will be able to fire an initial 16 rounds per minute and a sustained rate of fire at four rounds per minute.

The first production examples of the Model B version of the Stryker mortar carrier vehicle will enter Army service sometime in 2004. All the Stryker Model A mortar carriers will be updated at some point in time to the Model B mortar carrier configuration.

INDEX

**Hummer:
The Next Generation**
ISBN 0-7603-0045-3

**German Tanks of
World War II in Color**
ISBN 0-7603-0671-0

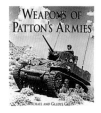

Weapons of Patton's Armies
ISBN 0-7603-0821-7

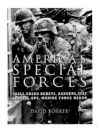

America's Special Forces
ISBN 0-7603-1348-2

U.S. Army Special Forces
ISBN 0-7603-0862-4

To Be A U.S. Army Ranger
ISBN 0-7603-1314-8

Modern U.S. Navy Destroyers
ISBN 0-7603-0869-1

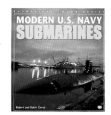

Modern U.S. Navy Submarines
ISBN 0-7603-0276-6

U.S. Navy Seals in Action
ISBN 0-87938-933-1

Find us on the internet at www.motorbooks.com 1-800-826-6600